NATURAL GARDENING
SMALL IN SPACES

NATURAL GARDENING
SMALL IN SPACES

NOËL KINGSBURY

FRANCES LINCOLN

Frances Lincoln Limited
4 Torriano Mews
Torriano Avenue
London NW5 2RZ
www.franceslincoln.com

British Library Cataloguing-in-Publication Data
A catalogue record for this book is available from the
British Library.

ISBN 0 7112 2015 8

Designed by Becky Clarke
Set in Perpetua and Today SB

Printed and bound in Singapore by Tien Wah Press.

2 4 6 8 9 7 5 3 1

HALF-TITLE PAGE *Lavandula stoechas* subsp.*pedunculata* flowers among daisies (*Bellis perennis*) with yellow-green *Euphorbia nicaeensis* on a bank of poor soil in my garden.

FRONTISPIECE *Alchemilla mollis* thrives with little attention, and its lime-green flowers offer a wonderful foil to many other colours. Here, they set off the purple flower globes of alliums. The climbers on the wall behind provide a good microhabitat for a variety of creatures.

Contents

INTRODUCTION

Imagine your own slice of wilderness at home: a garden that, however small, is a part of the natural world, where garden plants and wildflowers mingle, and wildlife feels free to come and go. It could be a kind of mini-nature reserve: a place where birds feed and nest, butterflies, moths and dragonflies are frequent visitors, and frogs return every year to breed in the pond. The beauty of plants in their wild homes is increasingly recognized, and many want to emulate natural places in their gardens. But how to achieve all this in a small space?

In an increasingly urban and built-upon world, the garden is, for many of us, the only place where we engage directly with natural processes – by planting, weeding or pruning, or by gardening to attract wildlife. It is our key contact point with nature. So the idea of a 'natural' garden is an alluring one. However, the terms 'natural garden' and 'natural gardening' mean different things to different people. Here are some of those meanings:

- an informal garden, where there is no clipping or training of plants, and no attempt to grow what would not normally thrive, so no varieties that need winter protection or other special measures to enable them to survive
- a place where something of the peace and serenity of wild spaces may be felt; a therapeutic antidote to modern living
- a place for nature, where human control is limited, and wildlife, such as insects and birds, can be encouraged
- the use of wildflowers and plants that have not been intensively hybridized
- a place where design is inspired by natural places and wild plant communities
- a 'wild garden' where only the minimum of intervention is made, and a deliberately anarchic style is encouraged
- the reduction or elimination of synthetic chemicals, and the use of 'sustainable' methods of gardening.

OPPOSITE A diverse selection of shrubs, climbers and perennials makes for good wildlife habitat.. A light soil is ideal for short-lived species that depend upon self-sowing for their continued existence in the garden, such as the foxglove relative *Digitalis ferruginea* (foreground, right) and the grass *Stipa tenuissima* (foreground, left).

All of these will be discussed to some extent in this book, but the core of the book is an attempt to explain how plants grow in nature, and how we gardeners can put this knowledge to use by creating spaces which are enriching both for us and for wild creatures. Our aim is to make gardens that encapsulate nature in a small space, and thus allow us to experience something of the beauty, the vibrancy and the complexity of nature.

The idea of a 'natural' garden is a paradox, because a garden is an artificial creation. This should not be seen as a problem, but as part of the attraction; gardens have always been the meeting places of natural processes and human desire and artifice. This book is about making a garden where there is a balance and harmony between human enjoyment and natural diversity. And it is about making such a garden in the relatively small spaces to which most of us are limited.

First and foremost it is essential to see nature as an inspiration. Nature is about close and intimate spaces, as well as big ones. This is something to think about the next time that you are on a country walk. Take, for instance, a wildflower meadow, which can be appreciated as a whole, or in detail. On hands and knees, at a rabbit's eye level, one can see that there is a great deal of complexity: a number of closely intertwined plant species, some tall, some shorter, some forming rosettes close to the ground, some leaning on others, some clambering up others to the light. There can be an amazing amount going on in a single square metre.

Some environments manage to fit so much into a small space that as observers we can almost lose ourselves in them and imagine that we are in a much wider landscape. These places can offer something of a vignette of nature and natural processes. Among my own favourites are pools in acidic boggy places with their variety of mosses, rushes, small flowering plants and dwarf wiry shrubs; ancient rotting tree stumps slowly being colonized by ferns, tree seedlings and mosses; and the short wildflower-spangled turf that you can sometimes find on poor thin soils over sand or limestone.

Some people find the idea of the 'wild garden' attractive. This is especially appealing for owners of large gardens where there may be places that are difficult to

Wildflower ecosystems are often at their most colourful in mountain areas, where a short growing season suppresses vigorous grasses. Notice the complex pattern of intermingled growth – quite different from the appearance of a garden border.

maintain regularly, and for owners of country gardens where it may be desirable to create a sense of the garden blending with the surroundings. For small gardens, however, and urban ones especially, a garden that is too wild all too often ends up looking an uncared-for mess. It is also a lost opportunity, as management creates more interest and wildlife habitat than lack of management. Simply 'letting go' usually ends up handing the garden over to the most aggressive weedy species.

Achieving a balance between ornamental elements and a certain amount of 'letting go' is key to a successful 'natural garden': art and nature are then maintained in a balance that is good for both. 'Maintained' is the key word. Perhaps more than in any other garden style, maintenance – deciding when to cut back, when to weed out, when to replant   is actually a major part of the creative process. Having a rich diversity of plantlife involves effective management of growth so that the more vigorous are restrained and the less vigorous have a chance to be seen. And from diversity comes interest.

The coast is a testing environment, favouring low-growing grey-leaved plants that can withstand exposure and salt. Here *Santolina chamaecyparissus* forms a backdrop to *Centranthus ruber* and *Salvia nemorosa*.

SOME WORDS

Before we go any further we should consider some key words and concepts. Understanding these will enable you to look at the beauties of nature with a more analytical eye, and to appreciate more precisely what it is we are trying to do in making a more natural garden.

Ecology is the study of the relationships between environment, plants and animals (including us). An awareness of such relationships and their complexity is fundamental to understanding our impact on the natural world.

An **ecosystem** is the complex web of life that exists in a particular place. One region may include several different ecosystems – for instance, oak woodland, hawthorn scrub and pasture grassland might be adjacent to each other, each with characteristic flora and fauna.

A **habitat** is a home for a particular animal or plant. The word habitat is also sometimes used almost interchangeably with ecosystem.

All wild plants form part of **plant communities** in which a group of interdependent plants grow together. For example, oak woodland charac-teristically includes hazel and ash, but not reeds or daisies; reeds, characteristic of

Many plants do not need anything that we would even recognize as soil: instead their roots exploit cracks in the rock or the gaps between stones.

a marshland habitat, cannot survive without higher moisture levels, and daisies need the high light levels and lack of competition only to be found in open grassland habitats. Particular plant communities are related to prevailing climatic and soil conditions. For example, oak woodland is characteristic of moderately fertile and moist soils, but not of very wet acidic ones. Plant communities are often very predictable: the same plants turn up again and again in each other's company over wide geographical regions.

Plant communities follow on from each other in a process known as **succession**. For example, bare ground is rapidly covered by short-lived weedy species, many of them annuals. This plant community is often referred to as a **pioneer community**. It is succeeded by somewhat longer-lived weeds and increasingly by various vigorous grasses, until a coarse tight sward is created. It is then invaded by rapidly growing trees such as birches (pioneer trees), whose seed is blown in on the wind, and berry-bearing trees, shrubs and scramblers, whose seed is spread far and wide by birds. Eventually the advancing scrubby woodland displaces the grass entirely, to be replaced after a number of decades by slower-growing woodland species, often dominated by oak, ash, maple and beech species. Eventually these species shade out most of the other trees, bringing the succession process to an end. The succession process is different for different climates and situations – for instance, open water is colonized first by reeds, then by willows, and then by alder and other damp-tolerant trees. But in nearly all temperate-zone situations, the end result is usually similar – mixed deciduous woodland.

Biodiversity refers to the richness and complexity of life. An old mixed woodland habitat, for example, will have high biodiversity, with a large number of plant and animal species. These take advantage of a huge variety of **microhabitats** – habitats of limited extent which differ in character from the surrounding habitat, and which might include woodland glades, rotting stumps and ground-level moss. Agricultural pasture has poor biodiversity because a limited number of grasses force out other species, and with fewer species and greater uniformity of vegetation, there are fewer microhabitats.

GROUND RULES FOR NATURAL GARDENERS

Making the most of a small space means becoming aware of the importance of including as many habitats and microhabitats in the garden as possible. This means more biodiversity, which is good for wildlife, and which makes it more interesting for you, the gardener, and often more visually exciting too.

Creating spaces that are attractive for wildlife is increasingly important in a world where intensive agriculture has greatly reduced the availability of habitats for wildlife in the countryside. Studies have shown that residential suburban areas with medium-sized gardens are now providing better and more plentiful wildlife habitats than many stretches of arable farmland. Imagine how much more space there would be for wildlife if all gardens were managed in a more nature-friendly way.

Another aspect of gardening in tune with nature is the use of plants that are appropriate for the site. Much conventional garden effort has gone into changing conditions in order to suit particular plants, with the digging-in of peat and the application of iron compounds in order to grow rhododendrons being a fine example of one of the more extravagant and in the end futile of these practices. Traditional gardening, with its historical roots in the growing of fruit and vegetables, where maximum productivity is the key issue, has also emphasized the creation of a perfect soil, which is all too often an unreachable and unrealistic aim. However, if your only concern is with long-lived ornamental plants, there is much less need to be worried about the soil. Plants are a lot more tolerant of poor conditions than we often think. Whatever the soil, the chances are that nature has beautiful flora somewhere for you to choose from. 'Difficult' situations have their own successful characteristic floras – just think of all those spectacular mountain flowers growing out of little more than crushed rock, or the brilliantly coloured heathers found on many cold and exposed hillsides. The 'natural' gardener, then, should choose plants for their suitability to the site, rather than trying to modify the site for the plants. The slogan is 'work with what you've got'.

The endless cycle of life and death plays an important part in nature and in the garden. Traditional practice has been to have little to do with death, and to clear up after it as soon as possible. Perennials are cut down in the autumn, dead leaves and debris are swept off borders and everywhere is tidied up. Yet seed heads can provide food sources for birds in the winter, and leaf litter can be home to myriad little invertebrates. The latter may not add much to our enjoyment of the garden, but they are part of a whole web of life, providing food for many bird species, for example. It is important, then, to learn to take a more relaxed attitude to gardening and not to worry about every yellowing leaf or dead stem.

Native plants are important because they form part of a complex food chain: many invertebrates will only feed on particular plant species. The invertebrates in turn feed carnivores such as this spider, which will itself provide food for a bird.

Even small spaces can be attractive to wildlife if they are planted with species that are known to be good food sources, such as the purple *Verbena bonariensis* on the right, which is adored by butterflies.

NATIVE AND NON-NATIVE PLANTS

Running parallel to the growing interest in natural gardens is the native plant movement. The movement aims to encourage the use in gardens of plants that are native to the area. It also sometimes goes further and argues that only 'native' plants should be used. This is a complex issue, which unfortunately is now confused by a certain amount of ill-tempered debate. To summarize the arguments in favour of using only natives:

• Some plants introduced into gardens have 'escaped' into the wild and 'invaded' natural habitats, sometimes eliminating local plants. A good example is the effect English ivy has had in the Pacific North-West of the United States, where it smothers native woodland flora.

• Locally native plants are well adapted for a particular area and the variety of climatic extremes that are likely to occur.

• Native plants support a host of insect species, contributing to biodiversity, but non-natives (or 'exotics') do not. For example, an English oak in its native northern Europe will support over 200 insect species, but in Canada only two or three.

However, the following points need to be considered:

• The degree to which cultivated plants escape and become a conservation issue varies enormously from place to place. Invasion by exotics is hardly an issue in Britain, for example, except in the case of non-aquatic plants. And the vast majority of cultivated plants have not become a problem.

• Locally native plants may be well adapted for their local area, but that is not to say that non-natives might not also flourish.

• There are plenty of examples of non-native plants that are a 'broad-spectrum' food source – for instance, buddleja (from China) is adored by butterflies everywhere, and for nesting and roosting purposes wild animals simply don't care where a plant is from.

• Not all locally native plants support rich biodiversity. Very little biodiversity is linked specifically to holly species, for example. Hollies, like all berry-bearing plants, will be appreciated by the birds, who won't mind if it is a plant of North American or European origin.

Some gardeners may want to grow only locally native species, especially if they are primarily interested in natural history and ecology rather than gardening. However, native plants may indeed be beautiful, but the vast majority of gardeners want something a bit more strongly aesthetic as well, especially if they live somewhere where the whole national flora has been greatly impoverished by the Ice Age, as in the British Isles. Also, in a small garden especially, it is vital that as much looks as good as possible for as long as possible and to achieve this gardeners do not want to be restricted in their choice of plants. Most gardeners, therefore, will choose to use both natives and non-natives.

If you use non-native plants in your garden, given the problems caused by invasive exotics, you should bear in mind the following points:

• Some areas have lists of plants which are forbidden because they are known to cause problems. You have a responsibility to find out from government agricultural services what is on the list.

In its native northern Europe an oak tree (*Quercus robur*) will support a huge number of insect species. While few people are attracted by the idea of limiting their gardens to native species alone, the inclusion of a few key natives such as this can make a lot of difference to biodiversity. Fortunately there is also an upright form, *Q. r. f. fastigiata*, which is ideal where space is restricted.

- Aquatic or waterside plants are more likely to cause problems. Never grow non-natives in or near water that is part of a natural water system, or in large artificial water bodies. Never dispose of unwanted water plants in or near natural water.
- In areas where there is a history of invasive exotics becoming a problem, be careful – use only exotics with a history of good behaviour. In particular, avoid species known to set prolific seed or which otherwise spread rapidly, and avoid berry-bearing species that could be spread by birds.

The use of plenty of native plants is always desirable in a natural-style garden, though, as it psychologically helps root the garden in the landscape, and can provide valuable food sources for insect species, thus enriching the local web of life.

SUSTAINABILITY

'Sustainability' is about our ability to continue operating without demanding too much from the planet's resources or overloading its ecosystems with pollutants. Total sustainability is impossible (at least since we stopped being hunter-gatherers), but it is possible to drastically reduce adverse impacts on the wider world. Conventional horticulture still operates in some very unsustainable ways – just think of spring in the garden centre, with all those plastic pots of bedding plants in peat-based compost. Anyone who wants a natural-style garden is almost certain to want also to reduce adverse impacts on the environment. Here are some key issues:

Soil inputs

Even though as 'natural gardeners' we intend to 'work with what we've got' and choose plants appropriate for the site, so improving the soil is much less of an issue than it is in conventional gardening, there are still sometimes situations when the existing soil is simply so awful that something has to be done. In such cases, avoid using anything peat-based, as peat extraction from bogs is an activity that causes great damage to an increasingly threatened habitat. Alternatives, often made from composted materials or by-products of the timber industry, are increasingly available.

Garden features

When it comes to features such as decking and furniture, wood, being biodegradable, usually makes a better choice than plastic. But, needless to say, the

wood should come from managed forests or plantations. Increasingly there are certification schemes by which logos are displayed on wood products to indicate whether or not the timber has been sustainably harvested. Another point to consider carefully is the use of timber preservatives. By their very nature these have to be pretty toxic to work. Conventional preservatives often rely on chromium- or arsenic-based chemicals, which may leach into the soil, and if they do will be very persistent. However, there are on the market a number of products, often based on copper, which effectively inhibit fungal growth and hence decay, but are less of a long-term danger. Another option is to use hardwood, such as oak, which resists fungal attack and decay for decades and therefore needs no preservative.

DOES THE NATURAL GARDEN HAVE TO BE ORGANIC?

'Organic' growing is a philosophy which maintains that synthetically produced chemicals such as fertilizers, pesticides and weedkillers have no place in agriculture or gardening, and that their use results in considerable pollution, environmental degradation and damage to human health. Organic growers believe that only naturally occurring products should be used. However, because this is a belief system, rather than a scientifically based method, it has an element of dogmatic inflexibility; there is, for example, no scope within it for using any synthetic chemical, however good the chemical's safety record. There is no doubt that the chemicals available to gardeners today in the industrialized world are very strictly regulated: we have come on a long way since the days when highly persistent and toxic products were in common garden use. There is very little evidence that, when properly used, the products available to domestic gardeners present either a health risk or a threat to the environment.

But do we need to use synthetic chemicals anyway? To answer this, let us look at their different uses:

Fertilizers

Research has shown that most ornamental plants do not need, cannot even utilize, the levels of artificial fertilizer that some gardeners, encouraged by the agrochemical industry, apply to their gardens. Only annuals and vegetables really seem to benefit. Most perennials and shrubs tend to respond much less, and all that extra nitrogen and phosphorus provided by the fertilizers only goes to help the weeds.

ABOVE A high level of diversity ensures that even if one plant becomes infested with a pest or a disease there will be plenty of others near by that will be unaffected and will continue to look attractive.

PAGES 14–15 Wildflower-dominated garden habitats require little maintenance when established, and if you choose the correct species for the location they will thrive with no need for inputs of fertilizer or compost. This Mediterranean-climate meadow is colourful in spring, dying back in the heat of the summer.

Pesticides

The heavy use of pesticides and fungicides is only necessary if the presence of any imperfection is regarded as a problem. A natural-style garden is relatively densely planted, with a multilayered effect, produced by the use of a wide range of plants. This effect reduces the negative impact that the odd diseased specimen might make – so if the bergamot has got mildew this year, not to worry, there is plenty else around it that is looking good, and the chances are that no one will notice. The naturalistic look can 'carry' more imperfections than more traditional and formal garden styles, which often depend upon monocultures of one variety.

Slug pellets

Slugs and snails can be very damaging to seedlings, vegetables and some perennials as they begin to grow in spring, and can cause local plant extinctions. Contrary to what many people believe, there seems to be little evidence that slug pellets harm wildlife, and sometimes they are the easiest means of control. There may be circumstances, a new planting for example, where careful use of slug pellets may be the only way to save large numbers of plants – the plants which, when fully grown, will be contributing to the web of life in the garden.

Herbicides (weedkillers)

The main enemy of the natural-style garden is a small number of extremely aggressive weedy species: nettles, docks, certain pasture grasses and, in some places, poison ivy. Particularly on fertile soils, these can rapidly overrun slower-growing plants. Many regenerate from tiny scraps of root in the soil, which makes their elimination very difficult; and many are effectively evergreen, which means that in areas with mild winters, and thus a long growing season, they have a great competitive advantage over herbaceous plants, which become dormant in the winter. By overrunning other species, these 'weeds' can seriously reduce biodiversity. Those with the time may

prefer to control weeds without using any herbicides, and in a small garden this is often feasible. However, those with limited time, or who are less physically able, may find that using carefully targeted herbicides makes the difference between a manageable garden and one that threatens to overwhelm them. Herbicides based on glyphosate (for example Roundup ™) have an excellent safety record and are biodegradable. Personally, I could not manage without them.

To sum up, there are a few occasions when it would help a natural-style gardener growing ornamental plants to use synthetic chemicals. If we restrict the use of synthetic chemicals to the absolute minimum, to those crucial occasions when there is nothing else that will do the trick, and to products where there is little doubt about safety, we are unlikely to do harm, and should not be made to feel guilty.

Dense planting, including species that are evergreen, provides an excellent cover for wildlife, as here, where dramatic foliage also maintains visual interest year round.

DESIGNING FOR NATURE

A garden is not just a garden: it is an ecosystem, a place inhabited by scores of creatures, most of them invisible to us. Living creatures are tied together by relationships of great complexity, and this is something that any gardener who wants to foster rich natural diversity needs to understand. A natural-style garden will not only reflect this diversity but will also look to nature for inspiration, in the aesthetics of the garden, and in selecting the kind of plants used. Being aware of which plants grow in particular natural habitats can be a very useful guide as to what will flourish in similar conditions in our gardens.

Large climbers like this rose are an excellent habitat for birds, providing safe roosting and nesting places. They also offer hibernation places for overwintering insects.

DESIGNING FOR NATURE

Interwoven growth looks natural and by providing good ground cover makes a safe habitat for many small animals. It also helps to limit the growth of unwanted weedy species.

The reasons for wanting a more natural garden are highly subjective, but many people increasingly want to feel closer to nature and that they are in some way benefiting the wider natural world. To have visiting birds and other wildlife is to be a participant in a world much wider than the boundaries of your property. A garden that supports a rich variety of life will become a part of that wider world, and therefore a more enriching garden for its owners. Key to natural diversity is the idea of the web of life.

All living things are dependent upon each other, for food, for shelter and for recycling nutrients. They (perhaps I should say we) are tied together in a web whose complexity is quite unfathomable. Nevertheless the basic structure of the web can be easily understood. At its simplest the web can be thought of as a chain of links, starting with green plants, which manufacture nutrients from carbon dioxide (derived from the air) and water, using the sun as an energy source. Animals, especially invertebrates such as insects and molluscs, eat plants. In turn, these may be eaten by other invertebrates – for example, small slugs are food for ground beetles – or by birds or mammals. These may then be eaten by larger birds or mammals.

The chain continues when animals and plants die, for they support a whole wealth of invertebrates that feed on dead material, and of course the bacteria and fungi that complete the process of decomposition. Then there are parasites, which feed on living plants and animals. In the web of nature, everything is potential food for something else, in death if not in life.

From this, it can be seen that green plants are the start of the whole web, as only they can derive energy directly from the sun and from non-living ingredients. They can be thought of as chemical factories, supplying a whole range of products that allow all other life to function.

Some plants support more of the web than others. Some support it so effectively that the gardener may see part of the web as a problem, as when slugs demolish juicy lettuces overnight. At the other extreme, leathery-leaved plants like yuccas or phormiums may support virtually nothing. Most garden plants fall somewhere between these extremes and suffer occasional, usually unnoticeable damage, as tiny creatures use them as a life-support system.

The role of plants is not only as food for the base of the food chain but also as providers of shelter. Birds need trees and shrubs to nest in, small mammals need the cover of low shrubs and perennials if they are to move around without fear of predators, while invertebrates find cover among tiny ground-covering plants, dead leaves and moss.

Once there is a garden pond, frogs and toads will turn up remarkably quickly. They eat large quantities of slugs and other pests.

Plants ceaselessly recycle nutrients, every leaf-fall returning materials to the soil to be made available for others. Some species are better at taking up some nutrients than others, so when they drop leaves or die, these can be taken up by other species, to whom they would otherwise be unavailable. This is another good reason for having a high level of diversity in the garden.

Many gardens that are not managed explicitly with wildlife in mind can be a haven. However, the web of life soon begins to break down if plant cover decreases. Wildlife disappears primarily because of loss of habitat. Songbirds leave if there are no shrubs in which they can nest or roost; woodpeckers move to find dead trees from which to extract grubs; and amphibians die without areas of wetland vegetation. Well-manicured gardens, with their uniform mown grass and borders where bare earth separates plants, while certainly not ecological deserts, are relatively barren compared with 'natural' gardens, as they have far less plant cover.

Clearly, the gardener can play a vital part in supporting the web of life. The less there is at the beginning of the food chain, the less can be supported further up. In promoting the growth of plants, the gardener helps boost the whole chain. And the more a garden is managed for nature, the greater the biodiversity it will support.

A hedge can provide a 'wildlife corridor', through which animals can move from one area to another under cover.

A GARDEN FOR NATURE

What, then, are the basic principles for managing gardens for nature? And how do they fit in with what we ourselves expect from a garden, as a place to relax in and enjoy? We need to explore the basic principles of variety, connections, gradients and seclusion.

Variety

Wildlife species respond differently to different species of garden plant, often in ways we find it difficult to predict. Berry-bearing trees and shrubs are a good example. Some, such as amelanchiers and many red-fruited sorbus, are gobbled up quickly in early winter, but some are left untouched until later, and some are not eaten until almost the end of the winter. The reason for this is that the ones eaten later may take longer to become digestible, or may be simply less palatable. As far as the birds are concerned this is a good thing, as it ensures that food supplies are available over several months. Lots of variety of plant species is therefore important.

Animal species vary in their ability to thrive in different environments. Amphibians, for example, need the proximity of water. So having several different habitats – for example, shrubs, grass, a pond – is important if a garden is to support a range of different creatures. The more microhabitats you can fit within each habitat the better. In grassland, for instance, grass cut short may provide one habitat, longer grass another and very long grass cut only once a year a third.

Connections

As we have seen, much wildlife needs cover, so that it can feel safe moving around without being spotted by predators, and in particular be able to roost and nest securely. Think about your garden in relation to your neighbour's from the viewpoint of a small mammal. The shrubs of a mixed border offer security, as do those of the neighbours, but getting from one to the other may mean crossing a lawn and running the gauntlet of potential predators. If the two borders backed on to each other, there would be a larger block of secure habitat. So if your neighbours have a shrubby area next to your fence, perhaps you should have one there too.

It is a fundamental rule of modern nature conservation that wildlife must have 'corridors' between protected areas. Gardens too can provide corridors on a small scale. For instance, even in a suburban area there might be a sequence of gardens, each with a relatively unkempt wooded area at the back, which could be preserved as a corridor for wildlife.

Connections are important in smaller areas too. Take a quick look at almost any natural habitat, and you will appreciate that there are multiple links between one area and another: for example, a wood will have trees, linked to the ground by climbers, with an intermediate patchy layer of shrubs, which then connect to plants at ground level. Imagine that you are a small bird, hunting insects. You would be able to move in relative safety from the treetops to the forest floor, finding food all the way.

Many human-designed plantings do not have these links. Instead there are sharp disjunctures between one layer of vegetation and another, as, for example, in a planting of trees arising directly out of grass with no intermediate shrub layer. This may be effective visually, as it creates clear artistic contrasts, but it is not 'nature-friendly'. The trick for the wildlife gardener is to design plantings that provide connections for wildlife but also have enough visual drama for the human onlooker.

On an even smaller scale, wild habitats are full of microlinkages: shrub to perennial, perennial to grass, grass to ground-level moss and leaf litter. Not only does this complex and multifaceted system of links create microhabitat in itself, providing living space for a variety of creatures, but it also allows others to move around. A gardener for nature should seek to imitate such tiny links too.

Gradients

In nature habitats rarely change suddenly. There tends to be a gradient, a gradual change. Look at the edge of a pond, for example. There is usually a transition from dry land, through an area of soil which is waterlogged, but which it is still possible to walk across, to a dense marginal vegetation of reeds and similar plants, shallow water and then deeper water. Each of these zones supports different flora and fauna.

Gentle gradients are important not only because they allow the full development of these different zones but also because they contribute plenty of transitional areas. Places where one habitat changes into another offer living conditions to many of the denizens of both, which makes them rich in plants and

A wide variety of habitats in a small space: a pond, hedge, rockery and border. Each supports its own distinctive fauna as well as flora. Stones in particular make a useful hiding place for invertebrates.

animals. For the gardener the imitation of such natural gradients provides opportunities to combine a wide variety of attractive plants, which will encourage a correspondingly wide range of wildlife.

One of the most beautiful and complex zones of transition occurs on a vast scale — the African savannah. The area where forest meets grassland is a chiaroscuro composed of a number of different elements: small wooded areas, areas of sparse trees amidst grass and open grassland. Savannah is the habitat in which we as a species grew up, so perhaps it is somehow genetically imprinted upon us to feel at home in it. It is a habitat which has inspired some of the best natural garden designers.

Seclusion

Those who wish to encourage wildlife into the garden need to recognize that what most vertebrate animals need is seclusion from possible predators, and that may well include us. One of the ironies of 'wildlife gardening' is that it is all about sharing a space we think of as ours with creatures who would be better off without us being there. There obviously has to be a compromise.

It should be possible to create seclusion, in which wild animals can feed, rest and breed in security, with 'corridors' of planting between one area of cover and another, and small areas which are well sheltered from prying eyes and ears. Even in a small garden there may be quite a few of these: the strip where a border backs up against a wall, for example, or the area below and inside a densely branched shrub.

DESIGN AND THE NATURAL GARDEN

So far we have been looking at the garden from the point of view of wildlife. But we also need to consider how to reconcile these considerations with a design that pleases us and fulfils our needs.

Landscape designers talk about several different aspects of space which make it meaningful for us: complexity, coherence, legibility and mystery. These are good starting points for a discussion on how to design a nature-friendly garden.

Complexity

Complexity in planting design keeps us interested, and rewards a long-sustained look. One important aspect of complexity is contrast — between different colours, for example, or different forms and textures. We have seen how nature also benefits

OPPOSITE ABOVE The well-planned area to the rear of this pond not only makes an attractive backdrop, it also provides cover for wildlife approaching the water.

OPPOSITE BELOW The blue hydrangea flower heads are sterile, with no nectar for insects. However, their presence brings vibrant colour into an area that is otherwise very wildlife-friendly, with many intermingled species and sheltering shrubs.

The dense growth of perennials along this path offers seclusion for wildlife, and creates a feeling of mystery for the human onlooker.

from diversity. Given the vast array of plants that are now available for gardeners, there should be no conflict between providing assorted microhabitats and creating areas with plenty of decorative interest. In particular, considering the long season of foliage, it is well worth planning how to achieve a good mixture of different shapes, colours and textures of leaves.

There is a further, very practical, reason why complexity is a good idea in the garden. It is a way of spreading risk. Traditional garden styles have tended to rely heavily on repeated use of particular plants for their visual effects: think of those historic gardens with their extensive box hedges or beds of nothing but rose bushes. A fungus disease that attacks box or a herd of marauding deer (which love rose shoots) would do great damage in a garden of this style. However, a garden that has a wide variety of plant species will not be affected in the same way. Pests and diseases are often very specific in their targets, so complexity ensures that there should always be something that survives.

Coherence

Too much complexity may not be a good thing visually; we may not know what is going on. It has to be balanced by enough simple, strong elements to give structure to the whole and create a sense of harmony. For the gardener, achieving such coherence means sticking to some basic design principles. Simplicity is one of these: planting may be complex, but simple lines and shapes for paths, borders, lawns and other features will act to balance the complexity. This is part of the appeal of classic English gardens such as Sissinghurst, in Kent, where relatively formal shapes provide a basic structure, within which borders burst with cottage-garden profusion. Focal points are another way of ordering space and thus making for coherence, as they act as 'punctuation marks' for the eye. Certain plants have a dramatic shape that makes them natural focal points – anything with a strong vertical shape, or dramatic foliage, for example. 'Hard' landscape features such as sculptures, archways and obelisks also make good focal points.

Legibility

For something to be meaningful we need to know 'what is going on'. This is a very subjective experience, and people 'read' gardens in many different ways, according to their origins and life experiences. Garden designers, however, rely on most people reading certain plants in particular ways – for instance, spiky foliage plants as being 'exotic' or 'desert'. Key elements such as these can be used to give the viewer messages about the garden. A wetland garden, for example, could feature the grass *Miscanthus sinensis*, which looks very much like a reed, but is far more suitable for the small garden. Planted around a pond it will contribute to the ambience of an area and suggest 'wetland' to the viewer. Similarly, ferns evoke woodland.

Wildness in a garden is a particularly difficult concept to communicate, because people react to it in very different ways. Traditional gardeners, or people from countries with a relatively recent history of ornamental gardening, often read a wild garden as being 'unkempt' or even deny that it is a garden at all, especially if all the plants used are native ones and not 'garden' plants. It is therefore very important to get across that the wild effect is intentional. Juxtapositions of wild and controlled elements can be a very good way of doing this: for example, some of the best natural gardens explore the creative tension generated between tall meadow grass and geometrically clipped evergreens.

Red *Aquilegia canadensis* and soft blue *Phlox stolonifera* carpet a lightly shaded woodland area. The aquilegia spreads by seeding, the phlox by creeping shoots.

Mystery

It is a fundamental rule of garden design that not everything in the garden should be visible at once. There should be corners that invite you to turn them, openings that beckon, half-seen sights that need a change of position to see them properly. A garden that uses natural elements is in a particularly good position to achieve this, as diversity and complexity ensure a constantly changing outlook. Keeping parts of the garden partly hidden will also ensure increased seclusion for shy wild creatures. A garden does not have to be large to do this, as even in the smallest garden it is possible to create mini-habitats with mosses, small ferns, rockery plants and other

naturally dwarf-growing plants, small gradations in light, moisture or soil depth supporting different species. Small gardens, especially urban ones, may have as much planting space available in the vertical as in the horizontal plane. This can be exploited by climbers, or by wall plants growing out of crevices. The smaller the garden, the more important it is to create mystery through the unexpected.

A LOW-MAINTENANCE STYLE

We have seen how in nature plant communities, if undisturbed, succeed each other (see page 10). Certain landscapes are the result of interventions that stop succession at a particular point: grazing, for example, keeps grassland from becoming woodland because any young trees that begin to grow get nibbled off. The basic task of gardening is an attempt to arrest the succession process at an early stage, so that the plants that we want survive, without the weeds, the grasses or the trees taking over. The degree to which the gardener intervenes is relevant to the design of the natural garden.

Traditional, very controlled garden styles require a lot of work to keep them looking as intended, as the elements, such as geometrically clipped shrubs or neatly ordered borders, are profoundly unnatural. A more relaxed natural-style garden will require less work to keep it looking good. The ideal should be to develop a style of planting that, because it emulates natural plant communities, is relatively stable, therefore requires relatively little intervention. Garden meadows are a good example, where a variety of grass and wildflower species grow together, needing mowing only several times a year. Contrast this with conventional lawn, which needs mowing as often as once a week during ideal growing conditions and, if it is to look 'perfect', regular feeding and weeding.

The key to a low-maintenance garden is to keep the soil covered with plants for as much of the year as possible. Exposed soil is profoundly unnatural, and serves only as an ideal seedbed for weed seedlings. Good ground coverage helps stop the germination of unwanted weeds, and provides continuous cover for small animals, thus ensuring a more diverse garden ecosystem. It can also help stop the soil drying out.

ABOVE Ivies offer shelter to many kinds of wildlife, but should only be planted in regions where they are native, as they can be invasive if they seed into the wild. The pink *Geranium endressii* is a classic low-maintenance plant, which effectively suppresses weeds and also has a very long flowering season.

OPPOSITE On light soils opium poppies (*Papaver somniferum*), lupins and feverfew (*Tanacetum parthenium*) can usually be guaranteed to self-sow themselves, creating a natural-looking scene. Very little active planting is needed, and hardly any maintenance other than the weeding out of undesirable species.

The light airy nature of this planting encapsulates the naturalistic style. Flower colours are strong, especially in the vibrant *Geranium psilostemon* at the front, but the flowers are seen as points of colour amongst foliage rather than as solid blocks.

PLANNING THE NATURAL-STYLE GARDEN

In creating a natural-style garden we aim to combine a rich habitat with somewhere that looks attractive to us. To achieve this, rather than leaving things to 'go wild' we need to design and manage quite intensively. In a small garden the key is to create plantings that act as vignettes, or slices, of attractive natural habitat, appropriate to the size, style and function of the garden. Since we want our garden to have enough complexity to be ornamental and interesting, as well as having good biodiversity, a priority will be to fit in a high number of plant species in a given area. Those natural habitats where there is rich biodiversity are therefore a good model for us.

Seeing wild plant communities and natural habitats as models is an essential part of natural-style gardening. It is also a way of training the eye and developing the imagination. Country walks and wilderness treks are opportunities to see which wild plant communities have something to offer the garden at home. While rambling through nature, we may be presented with a particular grouping of wild plants that attracts our attention. Such a grouping can be an inspiration for what we can achieve in the garden. This inspiration may be an aesthetic one, or more practical. For example, a colourful bank covered in wildflowers provides an object lesson in how different types of plants combine: how herbaceous scrambling species coexist with grasses and more upright wildflowers, or how a particular species exploits the cover of shrubs. One of the first lessons to be learnt from observing wild plants is the level of diversity that nature can pack into a small space. A really good north-west European wildflower meadow can have fifty species per square metre; parts of the Ukrainian steppe have eighty.

Needless to say, in seeking inspiration from nature we should not go so far as to remove plants from the wild. Certain wild plant populations, bulbs in particular, have suffered considerably from commercial wild collecting for the garden-plant trade. Wild collected plants do not adjust well to transplantation anyway. Small-scale seed collecting does no harm, however, although legally protected species and rarities should be left alone.

CHOOSING PLANTS THAT FIT THE SITE

Fundamental to any nature-inspired planting style is getting a good match between the ecological requirements or tolerances of garden plants and the conditions prevailing in the garden; this is also the key to a successful and trouble-free garden.

All plants have certain preferences: for sun or shade, moist or dry soil, acid or alkaline soil chemistry. Most plants grow best in the conditions in which they are found naturally – think of rhododendrons, which thrive on poor acidic sandy soils, or roses, which grow best on deep fertile ones. It is true that the competitive conditions of natural habitats tend to restrict plants to growing in situations where they can grow better than others, while in the garden, where most competition is removed, many plants will grow in a wider range of conditions; waterside irises, for example, will flourish in ordinary garden soil. Nevertheless nature is a good general guide.

When we follow nature, the situations that conventional gardening wisdom would have us believe will stop us from ever being able to enjoy our gardens – heavy clay, poor dry soil, steep banks, waterlogged ground – are seen not as problems, but rather as potential habitats. Pretty well anywhere is capable of supporting interesting and beautiful flora. It is just a case of selecting the right plants.

Broadly speaking there are three requirements for healthy plant growth: light, water and nutrients. If a site is deficient in one of these (or in the case of water either deficient or oversupplied), a wide range of plants can still be grown so long as there are good levels of the other two. For example, I remember visiting a garden next to a river with a damp, fertile alluvial soil, where I was surprised by the rich variety of sun-loving plants that were thriving under a beech tree, a place normally inimical to much plant growth. Where there are average levels of two of the three requirements the range of plants that will thrive will be limited to plant species that are known technically as 'stress-tolerators'; in shade, these will be shade-tolerant plants, in dry spots, drought-tolerant species, and so on. These stress-tolerant plants are the mainstay of gardens in which site and soil are less than ideal. When two out of the three factors are low, the range of plants is more severely limited. Dry shade supports only a few rather dull evergreen species; poor dry soils in sun offers much more scope, although plant selection will have to be vigorous. For many gardeners the ultimate horror is the shade below trees where the tree roots extract most of the moisture and nutrients, and little else survives.

Before choosing plants, it is important to understand your garden. Is the soil prone to drying out during the summer or getting waterlogged during the winter? Is it fertile or poor? Do you know if it is acid or alkaline? Is it sandy, stony or a deep dark loam? How much sun does it get, or wind, or frost? You may well need to observe the garden over a year before you have the answers to these questions.

This city garden is a peaceful oasis, where the plants need little active gardening. Where maintenance will be minimal, it is especially important to select species that are appropriate for the situation, so that they can thrive sufficiently to fight off competition.

Learning by trial and error is important; indeed, it is the way that the vast majority of horticultural knowledge has been acquired. You can learn much about your garden by observing what grows well locally, both wild and in other people's gardens. But only you can find out what will really thrive in your garden. Many gardeners get a great deal of satisfaction from experimenting with different plants. There is little point in trying to make plants grow where they aren't really happy. Instead, find a few plants that flourish and then explore the possibilities that they present. For example, suppose that you have inherited a rockery in your new garden in a humid, mild climate. Small rockery plants, or alpines, which might be expected to thrive are a failure, even in full sun. The reason is that moss grows luxuriantly in the damp climate, along with an annoying number of small weeds which penetrate and suffocate the slower-growing alpines. One or two wild ferns have started to grow, however, even though the site is quite open; their growth habit lifts their fronds well above the troublesome moss. So, try more ferns: forms of locally native ones, and non-native species too. You may well find they flourish, and if so you are on the way to an attractive fernery. Once this is successful, you may end up appreciating the beauty of the moss as well, and decide to keep a keen eye open for new species.

The natural-style gardener is always observant of nature's achievements. By understanding the potential and the constraints imposed by nature, and seeking inspiration in the kind of plant communities that thrive naturally where you live, you will be able to choose garden plants that will not only succeed but also look appropriate for your area, and good together. The section of this book on Planting Vignettes of Nature looks in more detail at a number of different garden situations, relating them to what grows naturally in wild habitats with similar environmental conditions. It is to these plant communities that we need to look for guidance, for the overall 'feel' of the garden and planting combinations, and for individual plant varieties that are likely to succeed.

REAL PROBLEM GARDENS

There remain some situations that are problematic, often because of human interference and the destruction of natural structures. Frequently we can make use of resilient plants that are able to make the best of these difficult places, because the environment resembles their natural habitat or because they are good stress-tolerators. Sometimes, though, the gardener needs to improve growing conditions.

OPPOSITE ABOVE Meadow grass and ox-eye daisies (*Leucanthemum vulgare*) flourish within the formal bounds of a garden that creatively exploits the tension between the wild and the tamed.

OPPOSITE BELOW Annuals, including field poppy (*Papaver rhoeas*), and the grasses *Hordeum jubatum* and *Lagurus ovatus* use the strategy of flowering quickly and setting quantities of seed to enable them to colonize thin, dry meadow soil.

NATURAL INSPIRATION FOR GARDEN PROBLEMS	
Garden Situation	**Natural Inspiration**
Acidic infertile soil	Moorland, heathland, pine barrens
Wet acidic soil	Peat bogs
Fertile loamy soil	Prairie, savannah, hedgerow, wildflower meadow
Wet fertile soil, heavy badly drained soil	Marshes, fens, ponds
Shade	Woodland, hedgerow
Exposed situations	Heathland, clifftop wildflower meadow, alpine meadow
Shallow soil over limestone	Wildflower meadow
Dry soil	Steppe, short-grass prairie, maquis
Coastal situation	Clifftop wildflower meadow, sand-dune flora

Absence of topsoil

Building contractors all too often bulldoze topsoil away, leaving an infertile subsoil, yellow or pale in colour. Rubble left over from building or demolition may add to the difficulties.

Some very stress-tolerant wildflowers, those that grow in the wild on limestone soils, for example, may grow very successfully on subsoil or rubble. Indeed, since weeds and aggressive grasses will not thrive here, wildflowers may establish more easily. The wildflower enthusiast may even welcome such seemingly unpromising conditions.

Rubble in itself does not present a problem, as many natural soils are extremely stony, but there may be physical difficulty in actually putting plants in. Small specimens will be easiest to plant, and in any difficult environment small plants always establish most easily anyway. Rubble is usually accompanied by mortar, which contains lime, so it is best to select plants which are native to limestone areas: small grassland perennials, spreading rockery plants, aromatic-leaved herbs and Mediterranean-climate small shrubs such as ceanothus and lavender.

However, many gardeners will want to grow a wider range of plants. In this case it is sensible to decide on a limited area to improve first and work on that before committing to working on the whole garden. Importing topsoil to form a 15 cm/6 inch layer on top is one option. This at least gives plants something to start off in. Alternatively you can work on the soil as you put in new plants, removing stones, breaking up the soil to allow roots to penetrate, and adding a mulch of humus-rich organic matter after planting. Humus will help to encourage the earthworms and other soil animals that are needed for the development of healthy soil.

Humid regions support an enormous number of different species of moss, which reward close attention. Though often underrated as a garden element, mosses can be a major source of interest in a deeply shaded habitat.

Compaction

Areas of standing water in places where you would expect it to drain away may indicate soil compaction, either surface compaction (perhaps caused by building activities or sustained foot traffic) or a buried 'hardpan' which impedes both the passage of water and the penetration of plant roots. Digging a trench will enable you to examine the soil and see where the problem lies. Deep hardpans need to be broken up with a pickaxe, so that water and roots can move downwards, whereas surface compaction is best dealt with by double-digging the soil and adding organic matter such as compost or well-rotted manure.

REGIONAL DIVERSITY AND THE SMALL GARDEN

An aspect of modern life that many people find depressing is the way that environments are increasingly becoming the same. All over the world one sees the same fashions, in clothes, architecture, car design, food and practically everything else. One would think that at least plants, by virtue of their link to climate, could

Light shade often offers, within a relatively small area, habitat diversity to suit a wide range of plants, from trees to ground-cover vegetation, with shrubs and climbers in between.

never be globalized in the same way as the rest of the designed environment. However, there is sameness even in planting. The same plants are used again and again in landscaping; in temperate climates, the 'green cement' of a limited variety of evergreen shrubs has become a byword for uninspired design. And just think of the fashion in temperate climates for the 'tropical look', which leads some gardeners to track down hardy varieties of palm and banana.

Neverthless, plants' close links to their environment and locality mean that they offer an effective way of counteracting blandness. Even a single tree planted in a small urban garden can make a contribution to maintaining a sense of regional distinctiveness. If neighbourhood and other community organizations decided to support a policy of co-ordinated planting, much more could be achieved.

So what constitutes distinctive regional planting? Trees are an obvious starting point. Particular trees tend to dominate in certain landscapes – for example, willows in river flood plains and pines by the coast. Even on a much smaller scale, a garden can forge links to the wider region through appropriate planting. Though there might not be much visible beyond the bounds of the garden, for users of the garden there may be a strong psychological linkage. An example could be the use of a particularly common or distinctive regional wildflower. The recreation of a slice of a local wild plant habitat raises interesting possibilities. For example, in an area where the surroundings feature pines and low evergreen shrubs, a combination of similar plants, including perhaps both native and ornamental non-native species, could be used. Apart from aesthetic and other subjective considerations, such a locally appropriate planting will be much more likely to survive any extremes of weather conditions that might destroy other, less regionally linked plantings.

Some lucky garden owners might have a view that enables them to bring a local natural habitat into the garden. The concept of 'borrowed landscape' is one that is crucial to Japanese garden design, and has had considerable influence on Western design. It is a way not only of making a distant view part of a garden but also of creating links between garden and locality. It can work both ways: a view visible from the garden may be incorporated into the design, and if plants are grown in the garden that are to be found in the view, the garden can be made to be truly a part of the wider landscape.

THINKING VERTICALLY

We cannot fit much into a small garden, which is a limitation, as a reconstructed natural habitat or a 'wild style' of planting often looks best on a large scale. Although with clever design it is possible to evoke much larger scenes, in a small garden we have little opportunity to develop the vistas and the long views that larger garden owners have. The gaze of the viewer is directed much more closely to what is near at hand, and detail and complexity – two factors that are crucial in natural habitats, contributing to a high level of biodiversity – therefore become extremely important for maintaining interest.

A key part of developing detail and diversity in the small garden is the vertical element. It is often possible to create plantings that represent or are inspired by nature on a vertical scale and capture something of the detail of wild plant communities, if not the expanse. All natural habitats have an important vertical dimension. So do gardens. In a small garden, the vertical dimension becomes all the more important as using it enables us to exploit a small amount of space to its maximum, as well as allowing more biodiversity to develop.

The easiest way to start thinking about the vertical dimension is with woodland. In nature, we tend to think of the trees first, but at home, on a more intimate scale, we are usually more aware of what happens on the ground. So, thinking from the ground up, bulbs and low herbaceous plants tend to dominate, and beneath them a layer of moss may well develop in time. There will be some larger herbaceous plants, and above them shrubs and climbers, often intimately intertwined. Above these are the trees. Though it is they that define the habitat, close to our dominant view is of their trunks.

Even a treeless environment such as meadow or prairie has a vertical dimension. Some flowering perennial or grass species are much taller and tower over the others, and beneath them there is often a subtle layering, with different species dominating at different heights and some even using the support of others to climb upwards.

The habitat with the most developed vertical structuring within a small space is the woodland edge. Here light is able to penetrate the forest from the side as well as

Looking out over nature: a meadow provides much better linkage to the countryside than mown grass or hybrid shrubs, and reduces the extent to which the garden imposes itself on its surroundings.

Light shade offers the opportunity to build up very attractive and intermingled dense ground cover using plants such as the *Ajuga reptans* and lamium varieties here.

from above. Woodland trees and other flora are in dense coexistence with shrubs and climbers, as well as with perennials and grasses that are more typical of open sunny habitats. Given the nature of small gardens, where there is often a dense patchwork of light and shade, this is the habitat model that is perhaps most useful.

The structuring of vegetation is complex even on surfaces that slope steeply. Observation reveals that banks often have much more interesting wildflower combinations than flat ground. This is because the slope tends to stop the domination of an area by a small number of strong-growing species, something that often happens on flat ground. Slopes encourage a gappier vegetation, which leaves space for less vigorous species to find a foothold. Visually, steep slopes are exciting, because they angle towards us, enabling a lot to be fitted into our field of vision.

Some adventurous gardeners have gone to great lengths to create vertical dimensions in level gardens. Drystone walls are one of the most effective ways of doing this, as they provide many potential footholds for plants.

In small urban gardens it makes sense to try to make as much use as possible of any vertical space, in the form of walls and fences, by growing climbing plants, or with shrubs trained and pruned into place and integrated with climbers. Additional vertical elements can add greatly to the amount of space available for planting, and also help break up an area into a series of more intimate spaces: a variety of freestanding supports can be used. Obelisks, whether made of natural materials or not, never look anything other than intentional, but they are a good way of including a climber in a border. Frameworks of trellis that jut out from walls or fences can be used to support climbers to create a more secret and intimate atmosphere in parts of the garden. Archways can be used to similar effect, while pergolas draped with a variety of climbers weave their own special romance. Arbours, made of natural materials and festooned with scented climbers, are the ultimate retreat.

SELECTING PLANTS

Plant selection has an important part in the creation of the natural look. Wild plants often have a very different feel from garden plants. This is because many common garden plants have been bred for various features that make them more attractive to a human aesthetic: bigger flowers, brighter colours, double flowers, variegated foliage. The end result is often that the proportion of flower to foliage

has increased, making the plant look showier. This usually has the additional effect of making it look less 'natural'. If we want to develop a naturalistic aesthetic in our gardens, it is important that we select only plants that maintain the proportions, and hence the grace and elegance, of wild species. Double flowers and variegation are both 'freaks' in natural terms: they impede the reproduction and functioning of plants, and in a competitive natural environment such mutations are rapidly eliminated in the struggle for survival. Additionally, some garden varieties are of little use to wildlife compared to their wild ancestors; double flowers, for example, often do not have nectaries, and so are useless as a food source for insects.

It does not take much experience to recognize a plant of wild origin compared to a garden one, but how do you tell when plants are just labels in pots in a garden centre, on sale before the plants are in flower, or names in a catalogue or seed list?

A pergola, which can support a wide variety of climbers, is a useful means of providing vertical habitat in the small garden.

Natural-style planting schemes will only look natural if you use plants that have the proportions and elegance of wild species. This rudbeckia may be rather too showy for a natural look.

Names can in fact tell us a lot. A straightforward scientific or Latin name consists of two parts, the genus name followed by the species name – for example, *Rudbeckia fulgida* – in italics. Such a name indicates that a plant is a natural species, in this case black-eyed Susan, a member of the daisy family, useful for its late-season yellow flowers. Occasionally there may be three names in italics, for example *Rudbeckia fulgida* var. *deamii*, which indicates that the plant is a naturally occurring subspecies or botanical variety with a few characteristics that make it distinct from the natural species. A great many of the plants, indeed probably the majority, available in the nursery trade are natural species or subspecies.

A scientific name followed by a non-Latinized name in ordinary type usually indicates a cultivar – for example, *Rudbeckia fulgida* var. *sullivantii* 'Goldsturm'. A cultivar, sometimes referred to as a 'form' or 'variety', is bred from a natural species, or picked out by a nursery from a batch of plants grown from seed because it has characteristics that make it superior as a garden plant. A generic name, such as *Rudbeckia*, followed by a non-Latinized name in ordinary type, without the second, species name, for example *Rudbeckia* 'Juligold', indicates a hybrid – that is, a cross between two natural species. While some natural hybridization occurs, these days most hybrids are deliberately created as the result of a process that is carried out in the nursery business to create desirable new plants for gardeners.

Whether cultivars or hybrids are suitable for inclusion in a natural-style garden is a matter for individual decision. In many cases they are suitable if they do not differ from natural species in their proportions and have 'natural' single flowers. For example, *Rudbeckia* 'Juligold' has the proportions of the natural species and is a useful, extremely robust plant, ideal for the wild garden. *Rudbeckia fulgida* var. *sullivantii* 'Goldsturm' (the name is often shortened to just *Rudbeckia fulgida* 'Goldsturm' or even *Rudbeckia* 'Goldsturm') is also very close visually to the natural species, although the purist might object to its slightly more compact habit. However, *Rudbeckia hirta* 'Indian Summer' is not suitable for our purposes, as the flowers are considerably larger than the species, giving the plant a distinctly 'unnatural' look, and *Rudbeckia hirta* 'Toto' is totally unsuitable, with its almost dwarf habit and large flowers bred for the pot plant and bedding trade.

DEVELOPING A SENSE OF PLACE

An awareness of natural habitats and the plants that grow in them can be a useful guide not only ecologically – showing what will be most likely to thrive in your garden – but also aesthetically – indicating what can be grown that will evoke the feeling of the wild. An important aspect of plant selection is picking out plants that convey 'a sense of place', in our case a natural place. Take a walk through any natural habitat, and after only a short time it will be clear that some plants are visually dominant – sometimes to the extent that they actually *are* the habitat, as grasses are meadows and heathers are moorland. These dominant species are the ones we need to choose to form a matrix for the whole, and convey a sense of the habitats from which they come. In other cases, it may be a subsidiary plant that is relevant to us. For example, large areas of woodland are dominated by a single species of fern at ground level, although of course the biomass is 99 per cent trees. Since we are thinking about small gardens, it is the fern that we are interested in. In the creation of a shady woodland-inspired garden, the addition of a few ferns, or even just one, will immediately evoke 'woodland' in the mind of the beholder.

Sometimes particular plant species or groups of related species visually dominate a habitat even though they are only a small part of the biomass. Bluebells (*Hyacinthoides non-scripta*) may dominate an English woodland, trilliums a North American one, through a brief spectacular display of colour. More subtly, however, other plants dominate over a longer term through their form and structure.

EVOKING 'A SENSE OF PLACE' BY USING KEY PLANTS	
Natural Situation	**Key Plants**
Woodland	Ferns, especially evergreen ones
Woodland edge	Deciduous berrying shrubs, climbers, climbing species roses, umbellifers
Wetland	Large linear-leaved plants that resemble reeds, bulrushes and large grasses
Moorland/heathland, pine barrens	Heathers, other dwarf evergreen shrubs, brown foliage grasses, rushes, sedges, dwarf (green) conifers
Prairie	Tall grasses, tall perennials, especially those of the daisy family (*Asteraceae* or *Compositae*)
Meadow	Grasses, umbellifers
Hedgerow	Deciduous berrying shrubs, climbing species roses, umbellifers
Short-grass prairie/steppe	Clump-forming grasses, grey-foliaged plants
Semi-desert	Yuccas, grey-foliaged plants
Maquis/dryland scrub	Evergreen dwarf shrubs, grey-foliaged plants

Umbellifers, members of the cow parsley or Queen Anne's lace family (the *Apiaceae*), are very frequent over a whole range of both open and partly shaded habitats in temperate-zone Europe. Historically, they, along with grasses, have been largely ignored by gardeners. Now, however, many more are commercially available, as their value as structure plants in the garden has been recognized. For our purposes their presence in the garden immediately evokes 'nature'; they, like ornamental grasses, can do much to create a more naturalistic feel in a garden.

Encouraging the onlooker to 'read' a garden or planting as you intend is one of the tricks of a good designer. Overall plant selection is of course important, and if

appropriate plants have been chosen for the site, there will, almost automatically, be a strong feeling that relates it to a particular wild habitat. Obviously if you are planting a small meadow or a heathland, it will be grasses or heathers respectively that will dominate and be the matrix for the whole. Less obviously habitat-orientated plantings can still evoke a sense of habitat through using species that have strong links with particular places, as, for example, ferns with woodland. In other cases, where the gardener might be more interested in an ornamental planting rather than one that consciously evokes a particular habitat, a few key plants can still make all the difference. The addition of two or three umbellifers or grasses to a border will convince nobody that this is a meadow or hedgerow, but nevertheless they will add a note of 'nature', both because of their distinctive loose texture and because we tend to associate such plants with a natural setting rather than with a border. Usually the most effective key plants are those that are evergreen, or have a strong structure or distinctive colour over a long season.

Repetition of planting, as with the crimson opium poppies and the grasses here, is key to achieving a natural look. Notice too how this planting has a meadow-like character: the eye is encouraged to run over it rather than to examine individual plants, as in more conventional borders.

DESIGNING PLANTING TO LOOK NATURAL

Only the most devoted naturalist (rather than gardener) will want to actually recreate a natural habitat down to the last detail in their garden. Natural habitats rarely organize matters as aesthetically as we would like. It is important, especially in small gardens, to have plenty of seasonal interest, with flowers or interesting foliage to appreciate for as much of the year as possible. Nature rarely provides this.

A natural-style garden aims to evoke nature through replicating natural patterns and habits of growth, and in doing so to create a habitat for more wildlife than a conventional garden would. Most of the plant varieties used may well be the same as would appear in many other gardens. Yet the way they are used can make all the difference to whether or not the planting then appears 'natural'. It is quite possible to take two garden designers, supply them with equal numbers of identical plants and get two completely different gardens, one appearing naturalistic and the other formal.

Conventional planting design aims to create effects that are very different from the way that plants naturally place themselves. In nature, plants tend to grow very closely intermingled. A field of wildflowers has its particular visual impact because a limited number of species are in flower at once and they are thoroughly mixed up in a mosaic effect. Individual flowers tend to be subsumed into the whole, in a visual effect similar to that achieved by the pointillist style of painting. Usually the mixing is not random, but involves drifts of greater concentrations of particular species in particular areas. Conventional garden planting, in contrast, tends to bunch plants together in clumps.

Unless you are making a wildflower meadow, garden planting always involves far fewer plants per unit area than wild planting. Plants therefore are able to grow larger, which makes the intimate blending of species that occurs in nature impossible to achieve and reduces the mosaic effect. This is particularly so when plants are clumped together. Clumping also means that only a small number of species can be used, and this is counterproductive to our purpose as 'natural' gardeners: we are aiming for variety and therefore want to include lots of different plants.

So how do we design a more naturalistic aesthetic in the smaller garden? The key lies in developing a sense of rhythm and unity in planting, two concepts that are often paid scant attention in conventional garden design. Using a few theme plants as the basis of a design can make all the difference. Theme plants are plants with a

long season of interest (which can be floral or structural) that are scattered around a planting, or indeed a whole garden. When repeated they create a sense of unity over the whole space, and a sense of rhythm can be developed by spacing. It doesn't take very many theme plants to achieve an effect. Three is a good minimum number for a small bed. The key plants for habitat character noted overleaf are obvious examples to use. However, others could be chosen because they have a strong colour and flower for a long time, or simply because they grow well in the garden and you like them. Sometimes theme plants select themselves. *Digitalis ferruginea*, for instance, a foxglove relative with a very narrow flower spike which has structural interest for many months after it finishes flowering, like all foxgloves self-sows, scattering itself all over the garden, which creates a wonderful link between the different parts of the garden. Being narrow, it takes up little sideways space. There is no need to sacrifice variety, as a few well-chosen theme

Knautia macedonica's long flowering season and tolerance of dry conditions makes it a very useful plant. Here the powerful red of its flowers stands out against the silvery thistle heads of *Eryngium giganteum*.

EXAMPLES OF THEME PLANTS

Name	Habitat	Characteristics	Season	Design Relationships
Digitalis ferruginea	Semi-shade or sun	Narrow spikes	Early summer to late winter	Adds vertical dimension to plantings dominated by lower plants
Polypodium vulgare (hart's tongue fern)	Deep to light shade	Evergreen strap-shaped leaves	All year	Contrasts with finer leaf shapes
Verbascum spp.	Sun, dry poor and sandy soils	Yellow flowers in dramatic spires	Early summer to late winter	Contrast with blues in summer; create winter interest
Knautia macedonica	Sun, dry poor and alkaline soils	Very striking deep red pink flowers	All summer	Rich harmonies with pinks, blues and pastel shades
Carex testacea	Sun, poor soils, exposed sites	Bronze-toned leaves, evergreen	All year	Contrasts with dwarf shrubs, and green evergreens
Solidago rugosa (rough goldenrod)	Sun, very light shade, fertile soils	Fine panicles of yellow flowers	Autumn	Contrast for blues and purples; creates misty autumnal effect

plants can act as an anchor for a wide range of other plants, chosen to relate to the theme plant by complementing or contrasting with it in colour or shape.

Theme plants can be used in three ways. One is for structure: the verticals of *Digitalis ferruginea* are again a good example of a plant that adds a long season of visual interest by offering a contrast in form to surrounding plants. Another is for continuity, offered for example by evergreen plants that have a distinct presence all year round. Theme plants can also be used for colour. A strong-coloured theme plant can make a basis for a whole planting, with all the other colours relating to the theme plant's colour. Indeed, in all three cases the theme plant can be used to set the tone for a planting selection, relating other plants primarily to the theme plant. This is a very good way of creating a plant grouping that will work visually.

AN EXAMPLE OF A PLANTING USING A THEME PLANT

This planting is for a dry alkaline soil in full sun, using the startling colour of the popular knautia (a scabious relative) as a starting point. Other plants have been chosen to contrast with, complement or harmonize with its colour, flower shape and habit.

Name	Description	Harmonies with theme plant	Contrasts with theme plant	Complementary Relationships
Knautia macedonica	Deep red flowers of a distinct disk shape			Sprawling habit
Centranthus ruber	Red/pink flowers	Flower colour	More upright habit	Contrasts with finer leaf shapes
Lavandula stoechas subsp. *pedunculata*	Purple flowers of dramatic shape; silvery compact dwarf shrub	Flower colour	Silver foliage	Bushy habit
Nepeta × *faassenii*	Mauve flowers on low spreading plant	Flower colour	Grey foliage	Neater habit
Origanum laevigatum 'Herrenhausen'	Deep pink flowers	Flower colour		Flowers later in season
Stipa tenuissima	Grass with very fine leaves and flower/seed heads		Fine foliage	Neater habit

THE ROLE OF SPONTANEOUS PLANTS

We have seen how plants that self-sow can play a role in the design of the garden. Letting the plants do some of the positioning themselves is a good way of getting the sense of spontaneity that we seek to achieve.

Many garden plants self-sow, especially those with a short lifespan: annuals, biennials, short-lived perennials. They make up for their short life by setting large quantities of seed, which germinates readily, exploiting gaps between existing plants. Those with a distinct habit are especially useful, such as the tall mulleins (*Verbascum* spp.) and the teasel (*Dipsacus fullonum*); these particular examples have a

SOME OF THE MOST USEFUL SELF-SOWING PLANTS

Annuals	Biennials	Short-lived Perennials
Eschscholzia californica	Digitalis spp.	Aquilegia vulgaris
Limnanthes douglasii	Dipsacus fullonum	Foeniculum vulgare
Nigella damascena	Euphorbia lathyris	Verbena bonariensis, V. hastata
Papaver rhoeas	Verbascum spp.	

usefully long season of interest too. Many, such as the evening primroses (*Oenothera* spp.) and poppies (*Papaver* spp.), also have showy flowers.

How much self-sowing occurs can be unpredictable, but as a general rule, the lighter the soil, the easier it will be for seeds to grow (this includes weeds, of course). What comes up is usually quite individual to the garden, however. Needless to say, some species in some gardens self-sow so much as to become almost weeds; the yellow mulleins are an example. Hoeing off excess seedlings is only a minor chore, though. In addition, most self-sowers have a very 'light' habit, taking up relatively little sideways space and not being especially competitive.

Some more long-lived perennials sow themselves around too, although very few to anything like the extent that those with a shorter lifespan do. Certain asters and goldenrods (*Solidago* spp.) self-sow, even to the extent of naturalizing themselves on waste ground. These tend to be bulkier and more competitive plants than annuals and biennials, and the gardener will need to keep an eye on them to ensure that they do not displace desired plants. Even some shrubs self-sow – *Buddleja davidii*, for example.

The subject of spontaneous plants brings us to 'weeds'. A weed is the wrong plant in the wrong place, which means that what is one gardener's 'weed' may be quite acceptable to another, or even that what is desirable in one part of the garden may not be in another. Generally most weeds share a number of characteristics: they are fast-growing and competitive, they spread rapidly and, despite the definition, most gardeners agree on what is a weed and what isn't, as few are particularly attractive and make the task of growing desired garden plants, or even native wildflowers, that much more difficult. Many species generally regarded as weeds are not natives to their particular area but invasive outsiders that can play havoc with attempts to restore appropriate native vegetation.

Some of the plants generally agreed to be weeds may be acceptable in certain prescribed areas of the garden. For instance, stinging nettles (*Urtica dioica*) are a valuable food source for butterflies, besides being an excellent spring vegetable and a source of fibre for handmade paper, and many species of *Chenopodium* and dock (*Rumex*) have seeds that help feed bird populations in winter, even though on the whole they are problem plants. We look at controlling weeds on page 153.

Conventional gardeners tend to see anything that they have not planted as a 'weed'. The natural-style gardener will have a more pragmatic attitude. There are many plants that appear in gardens which are not particularly aggressive and are attractive in their own right. In the right situation they can be a desirable addition to the garden. Some are native wildflowers; others are not natives but have gently spread through gardens from their original home. 'Benign weeds' might be a good term for them. Lawn daisies (*Bellis perennis*) are one of the best examples; they are attractive and, being small and shallow-rooted, cause no problems to perennials and shrubs. The more spreading Persian speedwell (*Veronica persica*), with its pretty blue flowers in spring, is another whose presence is often desirable.

For the natural-style gardener, who recognizes that gardening is a partnership with nature, many of these 'benign weeds' have a role to play in the garden. In my garden I find that some of them form an attractive border 'understorey', creeping among larger perennials and keeping the ground covered. They provide a microhabitat for invertebrates and a vital 'corridor' for such creatures to move around in relative safety. By keeping the soil covered they also help to reduce the space available for the seeds of more serious weeds to germinate.

Love-in-a-mist (*Nigella damascena*) is one of many annuals that self-sow. In regions with relatively mild winters, it will germinate in autumn, overwintering to produce sturdy plants that will flower for longer than those that are sown in the spring.

PLANTING VIGNETTES OF NATURE

WOODLAND AND SHADE

Many small gardens are completely or partially shaded, by trees or buildings. Woodland is nature's inspiration for such places: wildflowers carpeting the ground in spring, ferns and mosses growing lushly in moister spots, a variety of taller flowers exploiting those places where a little more light penetrates. The observant explorer of wild places needs to look to see what sorts of plants are growing at different light levels and in different kinds of woodland, and then to relate that information to the situation in the garden and select the plants that are most appropriate. Or the gardener may prefer to create their own small-scale woodland, which is possible even with only one tree.

LEFT In early spring, crocuses and the yellow aconite (*Eranthis hyemalis*) grow alongside snowdrops (*Galanthus nivalis*) and the leaves of autumn-flowering *Cyclamen hederifolium* – all common bulbs and tubers that thrive in the winter light available below deciduous trees.

PAGES 50–51 Moist acidic soil under a light tree canopy is ideal for rhododendrons. Here, hostas and a polygonatum species form a herbaceous layer, while below there are smaller ground-hugging perennials.

WOODLAND AND SHADE

Aquilegia vulgaris hybrids and the dark *Geranium phaeum* are easy to grow and rewarding perennials for late spring in light shade.

Woodland is the 'natural' vegetation cover for most of the temperate zones of the world. In the mixed forest that is the end of the succession process tree species of varying ages support a rich variety of wildlife. Growth is dense and multilayered, with scattered shrubs and a tangle of ground-covering growth below the tree canopy. Where elderly trees have fallen, light penetrates to the woodland floor, supporting a dense thicket of shrubs and young trees, all struggling to make the most of the sun.

However, most of the woodland with which we are familiar is not 'natural' forest, either because it has been managed for timber production over many hundreds of years, or because it is 'secondary growth', resulting from trees re-establishing themselves on abandoned farmland or from replanting. There is very little virgin forest (sometimes called 'old growth') left in Europe or North America. Virgin forest is instantly recognizable by the vast size of the older trees, the huge stumps and fallen trunks that lie mouldering away on the ground, and the dense vegetation on the forest floor. Secondary growth or planted forests are often in comparison poor in species and the trees tend to be more uniform in age.

As gardeners we are primarily interested in what happens on the forest floor – the wildflower communities that develop on a small scale. Different forest types have significantly different ground-level flora. Some trees, notably beech (*Fagus* spp.) and some maples, especially the European sycamore (*Acer pseudoplatanus*), are inimical to almost anything growing underneath them, as they cast a heavy shade and drop a blanket of leaves every autumn which are slow to decay and therefore tend to swamp any plants growing below. Other trees such as oaks (*Quercus* spp.) and ash (*Fraxinus* spp.) have a much richer ground layer. Birches (*Betula* spp.) cast the lightest shade of all. Most woodland wildflowers are slow to spread, so not surprisingly the richest flora is to be found in older forests, especially since they are more likely to have a patchwork of light and shade as a result of the trees being different ages, which provides a range of microhabitats for plants with different light requirements. Growth in lighter shade may be quite luxuriant, while the deepest shade may be populated only by a few rather dull species with dark evergreen leaves. Evergreens are able to make use of winter light beneath deciduous trees – consequently many shade-lovers are evergreen.

The life of woodland wildflowers is dictated by the need for light. Those that are not evergreen start to make growth very early in the year when the trees are still leafless; this gives them a month or two of relatively light conditions before leaf growth casts a deeper shadow on the woodland floor. Early growth is much easier if a plant has storage organs for nutrients, so bulbs and tubers are common. Quite a few woodland perennials are slow-growing, and hence in the garden require patience. These include some of the very finest, such as trilliums and the mysterious arisaemas, which have exotic-looking leaves and arum-like flowers. Shrubs, with the exception of a limited number of evergreen species such as *Mahonia* species, or semi-evergreen scramblers like those of the bramble and raspberry genus, *Rubus*, tend to be restricted to the woodland edge or glades where more light penetrates. High humidity, a common condition in woodland, favours the growth of ferns and mosses, flowerless plants whose small-scale intricacy and beauty repay close inspection.

Bluebells (*Hyacinthoides non-scripta*) spread readily by self-sowing once they are established. Their hazy blue goes well with the greeny-yellow of *Euphorbia amygdaloides* var. *robbiae*, a plant that flourishes in dry shade.

A species of *Tricyrtis* – a group of plants that are useful for colour in light shade in late summer. Like most woodlanders they need soil that is cool and does not dry out.

Crucial to the flora of the woodland floor is the distinctive humus-rich matter that forms the uppermost layer of soil, often only 10 cm/4 inches thick. Resulting from many years of accumulated leaves, and sheltered from the desiccating effects of the sun and the wind, it is soft and spongy, holds water well but also drains well. Many woodland plants have root systems that are very superficial, growing only within this layer and finding in it all the moisture and nutrients they need. Indeed, many of the most desirable woodland plants will only thrive where they can root into this type of soil.

Spring is the most colourful time, with bulbs and perennials such as hellebores flowering as soon as the winter begins to end, and in some places the forest floor can be covered by an extensive variety of herbaceous plants. The most inspirational spring woodland flora is perhaps that of eastern North America, where a number of species including those of *Trillium, Mertensia, Phlox* and *Arisaema* can be spectacular. Summer, by contrast, can be rather dull, although the variety of foliage shapes and textures is considerable – often more diverse than that of sun-loving plants. Late summer sees a few herbaceous species flowering: the white spires of *Actaea* species or the massed white daisies of *Aster divaricatus*, for instance, lightening the shade. The Far Eastern toad lilies (*Tricyrtis* spp.), with their interestingly dotted flowers, also bloom now, and can do much to make the early autumn woodland garden more interesting.

SHADE IN THE GARDEN

While wild woodland plant communities should be our inspiration, shade in the garden is often very different from that in the forest. Below are typical shady situations and some of the problems and opportunities they present.

Garden to house built in existing forest

The best shady situation, as wind velocity and strong sun are reduced, which protects the vulnerable woodland soil. These conditions should allow many true woodland plants to flourish.

Garden with existing trees which cast heavy shade

'Limbing up' trees by removing lower branches will admit more light and reduce the amount of moisture the trees take out of the soil. Slow-to-decompose leaves, such as those of beech and certain maples, can be raked off in autumn, to prevent them from suffocating plants. If none of these measures ameliorate the situation, the plant selection will have to be restricted to the limited range of plants that will tolerate deep or dry shade; these include ivies (*Hedera* spp.), butcher's broom (*Ruscus* spp.) and evergreen ferns like the hart's tongue (*Asplenium scolopendrium*).

Garden with shade from one tree or from buildings

Soil under a single tree is far more likely to dry out because of the wind than that beneath multiple trees, as there is little of the wind shelter that true woodland provides. Besides, single garden trees rarely build up the characteristic woodland humus-rich soil beneath them. There can be similar problems in the shaded areas of buildings if rain is kept off the soil by the sheltering effect of walls, or if the soil is of poor quality. Plants for such situations need to be tolerant of multiple stress factors: ivies, certain ferns such as *Dryopteris filix-mas*, or the wood rushes (*Luzula* spp.). On the other hand, if the soil is good quality and moisture-retentive, and there is no rain shadow effect, the absence of tree roots can make the shady side of buildings a good place for woodland plants.

Moist shade

Soil moisture helps overcome many of the stresses that reduced light levels put on plants. Where soil is moist it will be possible to grow a wide range of plants, with only the choicest woodlanders perhaps presenting difficulties. Naturally moist shade is a wonderful opportunity to grow lots of ferns, and perhaps one or two of the lush-looking large-leaved rodgersias, astilbes with their plume-like flower heads or the candelabra primulas. These primulas have layered flower heads in a variety of different colours, and a welcome tendency to self-sow.

MAKING THE MOST OF SHADE

Soil in shade can be improved, although if there are extensive tree roots in the way this may be difficult. If roots are not a problem, the organic-matter content of the soil, and thus its ability to hold moisture, can be increased to make conditions

Trillium luteum is one of those choice woodland floor plants that establish slowly but are worth waiting for. Here it flowers beside purple *Semiaquilegia ecalcarata*.

better for plants. You can use well-rotted manure, composted agricultural waste or large quantities of compost (perhaps from municipal schemes). A raised bed is a good way of containing and concentrating improved soil, especially along the side of buildings, where soil depth and quality are frequently poor; and where small choice plants are being grown, it helps make them more visible. Wooden retaining sides look most appropriate.

It is, of course, possible to use irrigation to improve dry shade. While I strongly believe that in most circumstances we should work with the environment we have got, and reduce our demands upon precious resources such as water supplies, if you have a small garden, with only dry shade, it might be justifiable to use irrigation to help turn a rather barren place into a lush habitat for ferns and other woodland plants. (For more on watering, see page 155.)

SELECTING SHADE-LOVING PLANTS
Foliage plants

Probably because of their need to capture as much light as possible, shade-lovers tend to have more attractive foliage than sun-lovers, and since there is relatively little flower interest among woodland plants after the spring, it makes sense to think about shade plantings in terms primarily of foliage. Hostas have traditionally been the favourite shade plants, but their large – and often variegated – leaves have a rather 'unnatural' appearance. Shade-loving foliage plants of some other groups such as *Saxifraga, Heuchera* and *Tellima* are more in keeping with both small spaces and a naturalistic look. Many of the shade-loving plants grown for their flowers also have good foliage, often semi-evergreen. Hellebores, especially the robust *Helleborus foetidus*, are particularly suitable for making bold foliage statements, while species of both *Pulmonaria* and *Cyclamen* often have beautiful silvery markings.

Ferns

As the visually dominant species in many woodlands, ferns are key plants for evoking this habitat in the garden. In addition most have a delicacy of foliage that makes a useful contrast to the broad leaves characteristic of many shade-loving perennials. While most ferns need moist soil and high humidity, there are some more robust species which are tolerant of drier shade. These include the chunky-leaved evergreen *Polystichum munitum* and *P. acrostichoides*, and the much more lacy *P. setiferum*.

Dryopteris filix-mas is another very resilient and adaptable plant; it is rather coarse in appearance, but some more delicate varieties are available from nurseries.

Mosses

Mosses seem to be completely beneath the notice of most gardeners, yet they offer in miniature a fascinating world of plant diversity. While most mosses are small, when conditions favour them they can spread into extensive mats that become important as garden features.

Mosses tend to appear of their own accord if conditions are right, but while they can coexist with very small flowering plants and some ferns, they may well be swamped by grass or other vigorous larger plants – making careful weeding out of seedlings an important part of moss gardening.

Bulbs and tubers

Plants that grow from bulbs and tubers are mostly very easy to establish, and over time will slowly spread. Bulbs tend to form clumps, so after a few years' growth the clump can be dug up and split, and the individual bulbs replanted. Some tuberous-rooted plants spread by seed, so keep an eye open for seedlings when weeding. Anemones and cyclamen are two that will self-sow. The natural habit of these plants is to form extensive drifts, either singly or in combination with each other, and for maximum impact, planting should aim to replicate this.

Various species of cyclamen can provide colour from autumn through to spring. Varieties of *C. coum*, in shades ranging from magenta to white, are particularly effective in the mid-winter period, and look very attractive next to the pale yellow of the primrose (*Primula vulgaris*). Snowdrops (*Galanthus* spp.) are the real harbingers of spring; and while to the uninitiated they all tend to look the same, the enthusiast will enjoy the differences between the many different species and cultivars. Crocuses come next, and then various species of anemone, such as *Anemone blanda*, with its daisy-shaped flowers, and the wood anemone (*A. nemorosa*). Later-flowering bulbs are plants of the woodland edge (see page 71), as they are not so tolerant of low light levels.

Much more easy-going than many woodland plants, Lenten roses (*Helleborus hybridus*) are among the most popular of late winter- or spring-flowering plants for partial shade. They flourish here alongside the fern *Polystichum setiferum*.

This species of *Amelanchier* flowers before producing leaves. It will later shade the bed at the base. This is a situation that is too exposed for many woodlanders, but where more robust ferns will do well.

These small early bulbs look good together, their colours complementing each other well. They are particularly effective when growing *en masse* beneath trees, and in some cases can colonize the weakly growing grass typical of areas under trees. From late spring onwards, their foliage yellows and the plants become dormant, allowing mowing to be resumed for the rest of the growing season. Small bulbs also integrate well with summer-flowering perennials, as their leaves will have largely died down by the time the perennials have started into growth.

Spring-flowering perennials

Of the perennials that flower very early in the year, hellebores and pulmonarias are the most popular. These are both genera within which there is a lot of natural variation, and there are now available a great many different varieties, nearly all of them still close to their wild parents in their proportions. Along with species of *Tellima, Heuchera* and *Saxifraga,* they provide plenty of material for imaginative planting schemes. All are easily grown in any reasonable soil. Somewhat later flowering are phloxes such as *P. stolonifera*, which once established can creep extensively.

There is another useful group of plants related to the familiar lily-of-the-valley (*Convallaria majalis*): *Polygonatum* (the Solomon's seal genus), *Disporum* and *Smilacina.* On the whole their flowers are subtle, but they are often combined with elegant foliage. These plants only really thrive in humus-rich, moisture-retaining soil. Such conditions are even more vital for choice woodlanders such as species of *Trillium, Arisaema* and *Mertensia*; there is little point in bothering with these unless you are confident you can give them the right conditions.

Late-flowering perennials

Upright-growing summer- and late-season-flowering perennials are more correctly plants of the woodland edge (see page 70). However, many will grow well enough in full shade, and can make an important contribution to brightening up shady spots. *Tricyrtis* are the most important, but they need humus-rich soil to do well.

Shrubs and climbers

Again, most shrubs and climbers need a modicum of light, and in nature tend to be restricted to glades, or places where a large tree has fallen and not yet been replaced. They too are considered in the section on the woodland edge (see page 68).

An exception, though, are a few odd shrubs which are genuinely full-shade-tolerant. Some, such as species of *Pachysandra* and *Galax,* are ground-covering evergreens hardly recognizable as shrubs. Others, including *Ruscus* and *Danae,* are more upright. At a first glance their dark leaves and stems may appear rather dull, but in deep dry shade, where little else will grow, they can be much appreciated. They are unusual and elegant and, because they are taller than most shade-lovers, useful for adding a variation in height.

CREATING A MINIATURE WOODLAND

You may decide to create a woodland area in the garden, perhaps because the trees will serve a useful function, such as screening an eyesore or ensuring privacy; or you may simply feel that the garden needs a tree or trees.

WOOD PILES

Piles of wood are a popular place to hibernate for small mammals, as well as for insects. As the wood decays it provides a home and source of food for a variety of insects, woodlice and other invertebrates, and they in turn provide food for other animals higher up the food chain. Decaying wood can be a very rare habitat in urban areas, or even in intensively managed parts of the countryside. Fungi will also thrive, and indeed it is now thought that decaying wood helps keep honey fungus (a very destructive infection of ornamental trees) at bay through encouraging diverse fungal flora.

But first, can we possibly talk about a 'woodland' in a small garden? The answer is, surprisingly, 'yes', although a few novel approaches are necessary. Traditional garden tree planting is orientated towards 'specimen' trees, often bearing highly coloured flowers, fruit and foliage, and placed in splendid isolation, so as to get the absolute maximum decorative value out of them. We, however, are more interested in evoking nature; and how often do you see a 'specimen' tree in the wild?

The best way to evoke woodland in a small space is to use several closely planted trees, choosing species that will neither grow too big nor cast heavy shade. In time, it may be necessary to thin them, even removing the majority. This goes against the grain for many gardeners, but in nature only a tiny proportion of tree seedlings make it through to adulthood, and by thinning you are only replicating a natural process. Alternatively you can plant several young plants of a species in the same planting hole, which will cause them to grow outwards, mimicking what often happens naturally.

Since the small natural garden must be conceived on an intimate scale, the 'woodland' must reward the viewer close to. Trees with decorative bark are thus perhaps the most valuable, as when they grow this may often be the most visible feature. Wild cherries (*Prunus* spp.) have wonderful bronzy bark and attractive flowers, and of course the fruit will feed birds in winter. Birches, especially those with good bark, such as *Betula utilis* var. *jacquemontii*, are perhaps the best of all for miniature woodland, as the shade they cast is so light.

Drastic pruning can be used to create miniature woodland. Trees can be 'pollarded' – that is, cut back at approximately head height or higher – to reduce their size and the amount of shade they cast. The results never, or rarely, look 'natural', but this may not necessarily matter, if their tops are not particularly visible. The bonsai enthusiast may even create truly miniature woodland, using dwarfed trees, with an understorey of moss and small woodland flowers – but that is another story.

Finally, it is worth considering the role of 'props' to evoke woodland. Piles of wood suggest forest, as well as providing mini-habitat for invertebrates and hibernating animals. Branches and other natural materials can be used in sculptures that also evoke wild places. Semi-rotted tree stumps are particularly useful; indeed, there is a historical genre of shade garden known as the 'stumpery', where dramatically decayed stumps, surrounded by ferns and other woodlanders, provide the centrepiece of the design.

OPPOSITE The ultimate example of small-scale woodland: a bonsai landscape, where larches and rhododendrons grow through a carpet of moss.

THE WOODLAND EDGE

The woodland edge is the meeting place of two very different environments. It is a zone of transition, between light and shade, and between the cool enclosed world of the forest and the open sunlit grasslands. Like all transitional areas, the woodland edge is home to plants and creatures from both worlds. It is visually rich too, with profuse growth of shrubs and climbers, which often form a dense and complex screen. It is this richness and complexity that makes the semi-shade of the woodland edge the key habitat for the small natural garden.

Various cultivars of *Anemone blanda* flower alongside primroses (*Primula vulgaris*) in the light shade cast by young birches in early spring. Both anemones and primroses readily self-sow to form colonies.

THE WOODLAND EDGE

ABOVE Aquilegias are short-lived perennials which thrive in light shade. Here they are complemented by the yellow-tinted *Milium effusum* 'Aureum', one of the few grasses tolerant of shade.

OPPOSITE A mown circle surrounded by woodland-edge planting makes a calm and restful spot from which wildlife can be observed.

Woodland can end in a variety of ways: abruptly, as when it borders fields or other open land; gradually, as trees thin out, to be replaced by grass and other lower vegetation; partially, as when a path cuts its way through forest; or in patches, as in woodland glades. In each case, there is usually a major change in the kind of plants that flourish as one moves from shade to light. The more abruptly this change takes place, the more likely it is that plant growth at the woodland edge will be really dense, in some cases impenetrable. One reason for this is that the woodland edge is not only a place where plants from two very different habitats can potentially coexist but also a habitat in its own right, particularly for many shrubs and climbers. This rich diversity of plantlife is mirrored by animal life too, dense shrubs being particularly good places for birds to find roosting and nesting sites.

Of all habitats, the woodland edge is the most highly developed vertically, from canopy trees, through climbers and shrubs to perennials and ground-cover plants. This rich vertical dimension makes it particularly suitable as a model for the smaller garden: nature shows us ways in which to pack in as much as possible. And smaller gardens often have light levels comparable to those at the woodland edge.

In terms of succession, the woodland edge is also a dynamic environment: it is where woodland is taking over from scrub or grassland. At its least biodiverse it may consist of a dense network of shrubs, which allow little to grow beneath them; this usually grows when farmland is abandoned. Much woodland-edge habitat, though, benefits from periodic management, which can result in a patchwork of trees and shrubs of different ages and consequently a gradient between different microhabitats. There is a warning for the gardener here: shrubs can grow large quickly and exclude other plants. They need to be selected carefully, and either thinned out or cut back if they begin to get too large. Trees grow too – indeed their unrestrained growth forces out most of the species that give the woodland edge such character. Just as management often stops this happening in the countryside, so in the garden the gardener must be prepared to limit the growth of trees if they are not to cut out too much light for other plants. Careful thinning-out of branches will keep light coming down to ground level without altering the essential character of the tree.

Small town gardens are often dominated by walls, which can cast a heavy shade. Here the walls are softened by climbers, and shade-tolerant perennials grow below.

The most colourful season comes later to the woodland edge than to the forest floor, with the main burst of flower tending to be in late spring to early summer, when there is plenty of sunlight but before a risk of drought. More light means that more competitive and faster-growing plants can flourish, so the slower-growing true woodlanders tend to be forced out. Spring bulbs are often a major feature, with wild daffodils (*Narcissus* spp.) being among the most spectacular, flowering just before the trees leaf. From then on there is a steady flowering of perennials which reaches a climax in early summer, with cranesbill geraniums (*Geranium* spp.), foxgloves (*Digitalis* spp.) and umbellifers often being the most prominent. Between the end of winter and early summer, a great many shrubs are also in flower, the earliest ones either being evergreen or flowering on bare, leafless branches. Climbers generally usually prefer to make some growth before flowering, with some species flowering in spring and others later in the summer.

Reduced light and, often, seasonal drought mean that summer tends to be a less colourful time; tree roots extract enormous amounts of water from the soil and there is much more desiccation from the wind and the sun than there is deep in the forest. By early autumn, however, as temperatures cool, there is a second burst of flowers, generally from upright herbaceous species, such as masses of white *Aster divaricatus* or yellow *Senecio nemorensis*. Later on in autumn, there will be a multiplicity of berries, a cornucopia for birds. Many of these are highly decorative, as are the seed heads of climbers and perennials. Finally, there is often a sumptuous display of fiery-toned foliage.

SELECTING PLANTS FOR SEMI-SHADE
Shrubs

Of the plants that thrive naturally at the woodland edge, pride of place goes to shrubs. Very limited by the lack of light under trees, they can form dense thickets in places where more sunlight breaks through. In the garden they are invaluable for breaking up and defining space, as well as for their flowers and fruit. However, since many shrubs get too large for the smaller garden and there is often space for only two or three, a careful selection needs to be made. Those that flower very early and have a good fragrance, such as witch hazels (*Hamamelis* spp.) and daphnes, are particular favourites for small gardens. Many of the shrubs sold for gardens – for example, those with variegated foliage, double flowers or lurid colours – are very 'ornamental' in a way that may not fit into the natural-style garden. It is best to stick to the natural species or those that have a simple wild feel to them.

Climbers

The woodland edge provides an ideal habitat for climbers: the growth of shrubs and small trees offers plenty of opportunities for support, while at the same time sunlight (the goal for climbers) is never that far away – certainly nearer at hand than it is below full-grown forest trees. While some are rampant, able to reach the tops of tall trees, many others are more modest. Most of those that are available as garden plants are woody – species of *Clematis* or *Vitis*, for instance – but some, such as the pale yellow-flowered *Dicentra macrantha*, are herbaceous, dying back every winter.

A clematis and the white-flowered evergreen climber *Trachelospermum jasminoides* cover a wall, bringing life to the hard surface.

Those with small or urban gardens, with walls and fences a major element, will find climbers among the most useful categories of plant. Fortunately climbers seem to coexist quite well, and it is possible to pack quite a few varieties into a small space – although they should all reach a similar size, otherwise the stronger will tend to overwhelm the weaker.

Climbers climb to reach the light, using a variety of means: tendrils, twining stems, aerial roots, suckers, thorns, or simply by leaning on other plants. Very few are self-supporting – among common garden plants only ivies (*Hedera* spp.), Virginia creepers (*Parthenocissus* spp.) and some hydrangea relatives. Support, such as trellis or wires, is thus needed (you will find details in specialist books on climbers). It is vital to know the final size of a climber before planting it. Too many

Bluebells (*Hyacinthoides non-scripta*) and yellowy-green *Euphorbia amygdaloides* var. *robbiae* have spread to form a resilient low-maintenance plant community beneath trees. The self-sowing annual *Claytonia perfoliata* fills up the foreground.

plants that grow 10 metres/33 feet are put in with 3 metres/10 feet supports; the stems then reach out frantically, grabbing anything they can hang on to. Big climbers can be grown on small supports only if they are cut to ground level every year.

Relatively few gardens show climbers as they grow in nature – clambering over trees and shrubs. Yet they can be very rewarding grown this way, with smaller climbers growing over shrubs and larger ones scrambling up trees, their flowering stems hanging romantically in swags. Since many climbers are summer-flowering, using one to grow over a spring- or winter-flowering tree or shrub is a way of getting double value out of a space. It is important to carefully match the size and vigour of the climber with the host, or prune the climber hard back annually.

Traditionally, self-clingers like ivies have been the plant of choice to cover extensive areas of wall, as they do not need training wires. However, recent developments in 'urban greening' have encouraged some property owners to grow climbers such as Virginia creeper (*Parthenocissus* spp.) or vines (*Vitis* spp.) up house walls on extra-strong wires or cables, creating a lushly romantic effect potentially several storeys high. Helping to reduce pollution by muffling noise, trapping dust and cleaning the air, this practice, known as 'façade-greening', has spectacular results and is even officially encouraged in some cities. You should seek expert engineering advice on the correct installation of such supports.

Perennials

Perennials play a major role at the woodland edge or in areas of light, open woodland. Most flower in late spring or early summer and can create magical effects, with highly complex combinations of flower shapes and colours. Many of the species that create these effects in nature are quite short-lived, exploiting gaps in the tree cover, as, for example, when a tree falls over, when there is only a period of a few years before the forest closes in again. Good examples are the umbellifers, whose creamy round-topped 'umbels' are a distinctive feature in so many woodland-edge habitats. It is worth encouraging these short-lived plants to resow themselves. This means that they select their own positions to grow, over time creating in the garden an artless naturalness which could never be designed.

Other perennials, though, such as the vigorously growing cranesbill geraniums and comfreys (*Symphytum* spp.), are solidly perennial. These tend either to form clumps which steadily increase over the years, or to run underground with

Lush ferns, bamboos and large-leaved *Rodgersia* species flourish in moist soil. Here they create an almost jungle-like scene at the verandah edge.

rhizomes or above ground by means of horizontal stems. In nature it is rare for a single plant to dominate, but in the garden this seems more likely to happen. Ideally we would like a carpet of many different species, all intertwined. In practice this may mean that we have to carefully manage the plants, cutting back or otherwise discouraging those that prove to be invasive over their neighbours.

Given this potential problem, the value of low creeping perennials such as species of *Ajuga* and *Lamium* is considerable. Early growing and early flowering, and low enough to combine with bulbs, they can happily coexist with many larger perennials, especially those that do not start to grow until the latter part of spring.

Bulbs

Woodland-edge bulbs tend to be larger and later flowering than woodland species. Some, such as daffodils (*Narcissus* spp.), have been extensively hybridized, so for

BIRD BOXES

A wide variety of bird boxes is available, but most are only suitable for a limited range of small species. Some specialist companies sell a wider range, for those species that prefer platforms, for example, or for larger birds. Books are available which offer plans for those with basic carpentry skills. Local wildlife conservation groups are often the best source of information on what is available locally.

All bird boxes should be sited well above ground or away from other routes which predators – the worst of all is the domestic cat – could use to attack the nesting box. Sites should also be shaded from the heat of the sun.

the 'natural' garden it is important to select varieties that retain the dimensions and graceful proportions of the wild species. Fortunately there are many available.

Some woodland-edge bulbs, such as blue species of *Scilla* and *Hyacinthoides*, form spectacular colonies. In nature these are often temporary phenomena, taking advantage of the gap between tree felling or thinning and the regrowth of trees or semi-evergreen scramblers such as the bramble. To get a naturalistic effect with these bulbs in the garden, you need to emulate these colonies, perhaps by ensuring that bulbs of one particular species are widely scattered throughout the garden.

Grass-like plants

Very few true grasses thrive in any kind of shade. However, *Melica nutans* and *Chasmanthium latifolium* are two which flourish in woodland glades or light shade and are highly decorative.

Many sedges (*Carex* spp.) and woodrush (*Luzula* spp.) grow well in light or even full shade, and their distinctive broad evergreen leaves are invaluable. In nature some species are dominant plants in their habitats, so growing several near each other will help evoke memories of natural woodland-edge habitats.

MAKING THE MOST OF LIGHT SHADE

The factors that create light shade in the garden are the same as those that create shade, but reduced, and with the advantage that any additional stress factors, such as competitive tree roots, are often less problematic. Buildings may still cast rain shadow, or soil may be poor, but the simple fact that there is more available light will enable a much wider range of plants to be grown. If conditions are dry, avoid plants that are known to need humidity or cool conditions, such as most ferns, waterside plants such as species of *Rodgersia* or *Filipendula*, and plants that are known to be slow-growing or have a reputation for being particular in their requirements for moist soils and cool situations. Vigorous genera such as cranesbill geraniums, euphorbias, Japanese anemones and digitalis are generally reliable.

Where lack of soil moisture is a potential problem, there is a need to be aware of the extra stress that close planting may cause, particularly where shrubs or climbers are near perennials. In such situations it would be wise to limit larger, woody plants to those that are absolutely essential; otherwise it may be difficult for perennials underneath or near by to get enough moisture to survive.

Where soil conditions are adequate, it is possible to copy the dense interweaving of different plant forms that happens in nature, and so get maximum ornamental value out of a small space in the garden. However, to really make this work it may be necessary to adopt quite an interventionist approach, thinning out or cutting back any strong-growing plants that are smothering others, in order to maintain as much diversity as possible. Below are examples of how layering plants creates a rich and diverse sample of woodland-edge habitat in the garden.

CREATIVE SHRUB MANAGEMENT

Shrubs are crucial to the woodland-edge habitat and to many gardens. They provide not only good habitat for wild birds, ornamental flowers and berries but also all-important bulk for the garden. However, they have disadvantages: many are simply too big for the small garden, especially good 'wild' shrubs, and the habit of nearly all is rather amorphous. Nevertheless, there are ways in which it is possible to include several shrubs in a small garden, keep them to size, make them more attractive and involve them in the kind of multilayered habitat that we want to create.

Certain shrub genera are widely distributed across temperate regions, with many species that are very similar but which tend to be characteristic of particular regions. As noted earlier, having some, or just one, of the species typical for your

HIBERNATION SHELTERS

You can help hedgehogs, and other small mammals that need to hibernate, to survive the winter better by providing them with shelters made of wood and covered with some kind of waterproofing material. Place these in the wilder part of the garden and leave undisturbed as much as possible. Hedgehogs in particular are major predators of slugs.

LEFT In the dry, shady conditions under the wall of a house, *Astrantia major* 'Hadspen Blood' thrives alongside the darkly elegant cow parsley *Anthriscus sylvestris* 'Ravenswing' and magenta ground-covering *Geranium macrorrhizum*.

region is a way in which the smaller garden can be linked to the wild environment of your locality. Examples of such species are given on pages 163–4. They may be available only for the geographical regions where they are native.

Pruning

Traditionally shrubs are pruned back from the top and sides, often with the result that they look like rather ridiculous and certainly unnatural 'bobbles'. A much more creative way of pruning is to cut them away lower down. By removing lower branches it is possible to make the profile of a shrub narrower and more elegant. All too often shrubs have attractive bark or stems or an elegant branching habit that is never appreciated until some drastic pruning is done. Cutting away lower stems allows more light to get to the base, making more habitat for ground-level perennials, while leaving a limited number of upper branches to develop naturally allows the inherent character of the plant to show through.

Wall shrubs

Conventionally used for training tender species to warm walls, the following technique can be applied to any shrub and is particularly useful for a species whose flowers are valued but which gets very large or ungainly. Plant the shrub close to a fence or wall, tie the stems to support such as trellis or wires, and remove stems that grow outwards. You can then grow small-growing climbers through it and plant perennials at the base. Growing shrubs by this method is a way of fitting in a narrow slice of woodland-edge habitat in a tight spot.

Coppicing

Adapted from a traditional forestry practice, this is a technique with enormous ornamental potential. The stems of trees or shrubs which are known to send up shoots from the base are cut back to ground level every other year, or even annually. The plant's response is to send up a number of stems and to produce leaves that are often 50 per cent larger than normal. It is even possible to use large forest trees: tulip tree (*Liriodendron tulipifera*) is an excellent subject as the leaves are so magnificent. In nature, coppice is an excellent wildflower habitat, but this is partly dependent upon the cutting being done on a twenty-five-year cycle, which allows for a steady succession from one plant community to another, from sun-loving species at the beginning of the cycle to

shade-tolerant species at the end. For ornamental purposes in the garden, however, coppice needs to be managed more intensively, cutting back being done every two to three years or even annually. Coppicing is a good way of controlling ornamental shrubs or small trees that tend to sucker, which is a most undesirable tendency in a small garden. Species of *Rhus*, which are notorious for suckering but which have attractive foliage, can be turned into far more tractable garden plants through annual cutting back.

A wide range of woodland-edge perennials of sunny or lightly shaded habitats will grow with coppiced shrubs. Those perennials with a low to medium height clump-forming tendency are the most suitable – they will fit in neatly under the arching stems of the shrubs. But it is the dramatic effects that become possible when shrub foliage is combined with perennials that can make coppicing such an exciting concept for the small garden. For a striking harmony try underplanting shrubs with purple or bronze foliage such as *Cotinus coggygria* 'Royal Purple' with blue-flowering cranesbill geraniums, or shrubs with rich autumn leaf colour, such as rhus, amelanchier or aronia, with late-flowering yellow rudbeckias.

HEDGEROWS

Hedges are densely planted, regularly pruned trees and shrubs. In agriculture-dominated areas country hedges, often of great antiquity, can act as refuges for a wide variety of wildflowers. Their value for wild flora and fauna is that they offer a transition from a woodland-floor habitat to an open one in a very confined space, and this results in potentially very high levels of biodiversity. In the garden too they can be used to support biodiversity. An informal hedge can be made from a number of species, some chosen for evergreen foliage and others for flowers or berries, some primarily ornamental, others there mainly for wildlife value. Small climbers such as clematis and wild roses can be incorporated in the basic structure. In a small garden a miniature hedge-type planting, perhaps including only three or four shrubs, could be used as the centrepiece of a border.

The base of a hedge usually supports a rich variety of wildflowers. In the garden a range of robust low-growing and clump-forming perennials can be planted once the hedge is established.

Rudbeckia fulgida makes a vibrant combination with the autumn leaf colour of *Rhus typhina* in a coppice planting. The rhus is notorious for suckering, but when it is grown alongside perennials and cut back every year this becomes much less of a problem.

GRASSLAND: MEADOW AND

PRAIRIE

For many people, meadows and prairies are the quintessential and most romantic wildflower habitat, places where there are myriad sun-soaked and wind-combed wildflowers. The romance is perhaps to do with the sheer richness of all those wildflowers and, on closer examination, all the different kinds of grasses as well. Childhood and memory play a role in our liking for grassland too; many of us remember playing in long grass as children, and we tend to link its memory to lazy summer days.

A field of wildflowers is many people's idea of a meadow. In reality cornfield wildflowers are a short-lived phenomenon, but they are very useful for making a splash in a new garden, or for interweaving between slower-growing but more permanent plants.

GRASSLAND: MEADOW AND PRAIRIE

ABOVE Yellow loosestrife (*Lysimachia punctata*) is one of the few garden perennials that can compete with rough grass. Here it grows alongside *Leucanthemum vulgare* and a few *Aquilegia vulgaris*.

OPPOSITE This prairie – in its second year after being sown from seed – is dominated by yellow *Rudbeckia fulgida* (foreground), *Ratibida pinnata*, which has reflexed yellow petals, and pink *Echinacea purpurea*.

Meadows and prairies are not the easiest habitats to recreate in the garden, in small spaces especially. But it is possible to reproduce them, and once achieved such habitats can be immensely rewarding. As complex and dynamic plant communities, meadows and prairies tend to be in a state of constant flux, with the proportion of wildflowers at least slightly different from one year to another – a rather special feature in itself. There is a level at which developments are beyond our control, but for gardeners who have made successful wildflower meadows that is part of the attraction – the unpredictability and sheer independence of spirit of the genuinely wild and untamed.

Humans and grass have always had a close relationship; after all, we evolved as a species in the savannah grass of Africa. And many supposedly natural grasslands are really only semi-natural: meadows are maintained by mowing, pastures by grazing and much of the North American prairie by fire. Mowing and burning eliminate tree and shrub seedlings, which in the normal process of succession would replace the grass over the years. Humans, often dependent upon cattle, have always tended to favour grass over trees, and have therefore encouraged the extension of the world's grasslands. These wild or semi-natural grasslands arc very often very species-rich, with thirty to eighty species per square metre being not unusual. By contrast, domestic lawns are incredibly poor, with barely half a dozen grass species.

Conventional lawns are humankind's domestic version of grassland. Generally, I think that as natural gardeners we need to question whether we should go to the trouble of maintaining such a biologically sterile and resource-hungry feature. But where a garden needs a lawn, perhaps as a foreground for the rest of the garden or for a particular purpose, such as playing games, we should consider alternatives that include more wildflower species and richer biodiversity.

Traditional hay meadows, steppe grasslands (or the short-grass prairie of North America) and tall-grass prairie are species-rich, wildlife-friendly and visually appealing habitats that can be models for garden grasslands. Indeed, most of the research and promotion of 'natural gardens' has been concerned with these grassland habitats. Grasslands typically have a matrix of grass, which usually consists of several key species, and a number of other, generally perennial,

'wildflower' species – known as 'forbs'. The proportion of grasses is generally 70–90 per cent. As gardeners we tend to want more of the colourful forbs. Too many, however, and the grassland may not function well ecologically, allowing unwanted weedy species to infiltrate. The mixture of grasses and forbs is also a vital part of the aesthetic of grasslands: the neutral green and fawn tones of the grass separate the wide variety of forb flower colours, as well as creating a characteristic sense of airy lightness. Both groups of plants provide a rich supply of food for wild birds in wintertime: seed heads and the insects that pupate or hibernate in them.

Grassland is fundamentally different from many other habitats, because of its complexity. It is important to take a while to appreciate this. Look at an area of wild meadow or prairie, and try to locate an individual plant. It is actually quite difficult. You will probably have to get down on hands and knees and pull grasses and wildflowers aside to see where one ends and another begins. There are no discrete boundaries; individual plants and species are intimately intermingled, growing into each other, around each other and supporting each other – totally enmeshed. Compare such an area with a forest floor, where many plants stand out immediately as individuals, where some form extensive colonies and where, even if they are mingled, it is usually easy to separate them visually. This complexity means that it is difficult to cultivate individual plants in a grassland; just as in maintaining a lawn, where all the individual plants are mown, fed and watered together, in a grassland all the plants are cultivated together and the amount of individual care and attention it is possible to give is quite limited. The success of a grassland habitat will depend much more on ecological processes. Our role as gardeners is therefore to set the scene and provide the right conditions for nature to run its course.

The reason for this complexity, and all that follows from it, is that, compared to many other habitats, grasslands are highly favoured with resources: sunlight, moisture and nutrients. This means that they are extremely competitive environments, in which a great many plants jostle for space. Contrast such an

LEFT You can produce an annual meadow by sowing, in the spring, a variety of summer-flowering species such as *Ammi majus*, field poppies (*Papaver rhoeas*), cornflowers (*Centaurea cyanus*), corn marigolds (*Xanthophthalmum segetum*) and the red flax *Linum grandiflorum* var. *rubrum*. Some will self-sow, but the seeds will only germinate – and give a good effect the year after – if the ground is broken up by cultivation.

ABOVE A perennial wildflower meadow, with *Leucanthemum vulgare*.

BELOW Yellow *Anthyllis vulneraria* is best grown on thin soils, as it can spread aggressively in fertile ground.

environment with a conventional garden border, where plants are grown at much greater distances from each other than they ever would be in nature. This competition is one reason why the composition of grasslands can vary so much, both between neighbouring areas and from year to year. There is also always the danger that one species will dominate, to the detriment of others.

Finally, it should be pointed out that the terms 'meadow' and 'prairie' are sometimes used for wild-style border plantings. Since such borders do not have the dense grass matrix of true grasslands, but have instead the relatively wide spacing of the conventional border, these usages are incorrect. However, these nature-inspired borders have an important role to play in the modern garden; they are considered on pages 120–35.

Purple-flowered alliums make an interesting – although short-term – addition to a meadow. The mown strips here emphasize the fact that the longer grass is intentional.

PLANNING AND CREATING MINIATURE GRASSLANDS

To prevent long grass in the garden from appearing, as it so often does, uncared for and unkempt, it is vital that a grassland area in a small garden is given meaning. It must look as if it is the result of intention, rather than a lack of care. This can be done in several ways:

• Mowing around, or mowing through, a meadow area, so combining conventional mown lawn with meadow, makes the longer grass and wildflowers look intended.

• If a garden has a wild-looking backdrop, such as an informal hedge, shrubbery or woodland, a long grass area can be a foreground to it. The eye will see it as a transition from 'tidy' garden to a wilder place.

• While small areas of long meadow grass can be visually successful, the longer the grass, the more difficult it can be to make it look right. Hiding the base of taller grassy vegetation can be effective: decking and tall-grass prairie, for example, make a striking combination.

• As a general rule, the shorter the meadow community, the easier it will be to fit it visually into a small space. Even a meadow as small as 25 square cm/10 square inches surrounded by mown lawn can be successful, but only with lower-growing wildflowers.

• Taller meadow or prairie looks better in a narrow strip than a small patch, especially if it makes a backdrop to trees, shrubs or a view. Even a strip 50 cm/20 inches wide can be quite striking.

MEADOWS

Strictly speaking, a meadow is a field that is mown on a regular basis, with hay being removed to be fed to animals. In practice the term is often applied to any wildflower-rich grassy habitat, especially in Europe. In North America, it is used even more loosely: this is largely a result of the marketing of the type of commercial seed mixes described overleaf, many of which will not form stable or even particularly attractive plant communities in the long term. In a North American context it is perhaps best to restrict its use to grass and forb combinations in those states that are outside the true prairie belt.

A buttercup-dominated patch of 'mini-meadow' breaks what could otherwise be the monotony of closely mown grass.

European meadows illustrate an ecological feature that many gardeners find counter-intuitive: the poorer the soil, the better the flora. Fertile soils, especially if moist, are dominated by a limited number of aggressive grass species, and comparatively few decorative forb species are able to compete. Modern agriculture, with its emphasis on productivity at all costs, has caused massive ecological impoverishment of European grasslands, as nitrogen fertilizers encourage grasses (and weeds) at the expense of wildflowers. On the other hand, less fertile soils, especially if seasonally dry, do not provide a good habitat for the strong-growing grasses and will support a rich diversity of attractive forbs. The best wildflower meadows are to be found on thin dry soils overlaying limestone, their sparse turf spangled with colourful flowers. Mountain regions have good wildflower meadows, as the poor soil and short growing season limits the growth of competitive grasses. Traditionally managed hay meadows, where nothing but manure is used as a fertilizer, often have rich flora too.

For many gardeners this lesson — that for meadows fertile soil is bad and poor soil is good — may be very good news. A town garden with a lot of rubble in the ground will probably be quite calcareous, and possibly low in fertility, so making it perfect for a wide range of limestone meadow wildflowers. But if you have 'good' soil you will be much more limited as to what kind of meadow you can achieve. You will be restricted to spring bulbs and wildflowers, such as cowslip (*Primula veris*), which flower before the grasses make extensive growth, and a small number of vigorous wildflowers that can compete with grass. Or you could consider a grassland habitat that thrives on fertility – the American prairie (see page 89).

On a small scale, both meadows and prairies can be created by sowing (the usual method) or by planting nursery-grown plants – see below. Sowing and planting are often combined, with grass being sown and wildflowers inserted as plants.

CREATING MEADOWS
Selecting species

There is now a wide variety of meadow seed mixes available, for a number of different soil types. Those for low-nutrient soils, such as limestone-based or sandy ones, generally have the highest number of species. Increasingly, meadow seed mixes are being marketed for particular geographical regions, partly in order to reflect local flora, and also to ensure that seed of local origin is used. This may be important for some species, which have evolved local genetically distinct races adapted to make the best of local climatic conditions.

However, not all seed mixes available are necessarily appropriate for a particular area and some are highly marketed mixtures aimed at a quick decorative result rather than a long-term stable habitat. Some of the mixes sold in ornamental containers have a high proportion of annuals, which give a fine show the first year, and little for future years. Others mix species from a wide variety of geographical and climate zones.

Some seed companies offer a seed mixture consisting of wildflowers only – that is, without the approximately 80 per cent grass content that forms a meadow matrix. The result will be very colourful, but without the grass it will not be a meadow. This means that it will not be a very stable plant community: it will be open to infiltration by aggressive weedy species, rapidly spreading pasture grasses especially. On fertile soils this may mean a rapid demise for the meadow if invaders are not weeded out. However, on very infertile soils, or on sites where a thick layer of sand (at least 20 cm/8 inches deep) is used, or any other low-nutrient rooting medium such as crushed hardcore, a wildflower-only mix may not be such a problem. Some experienced wildflower growers claim that, over time, a limited

number of grass species establish, but because conditions are not favourable to them they do not become a problem, and gradually an ecologically stable wildflower/grass community develops.

In regions where there is no native grassland, or in very urban situations, using locally native species may have little meaning or relevance; however, gardeners with strictly ecological concerns will probably be keen to grow a meadow only with species that would naturally occur together and in the locality of the garden.

Rather than relying on 'ornamental meadow' mixtures, I would recommend sending off for the seed lists of companies who specialize in wildflower meadow or prairie seed. Their catalogues and websites are often a mine of information. Most suppliers have a variety of different seed mixes, often designed for particular soil types and sometimes for different visual effects, such as season of peak flowering or height.

When planting a meadow from established plants or plugs (see below), it is wise to consider two points. One is how to obtain a grass matrix, and the other is the wildflower species to be chosen. The best way of doing this is to look at the composition of a seed mixture for your soil type and use that as a guide, but perhaps skew the selection towards the most decorative species. For very small meadows, bear in mind that larger wildflowers may take up quite a lot of space.

There is, of course, no reason why you should not be creative and experimental and add 'garden perennials' to a wildflower meadow in the garden. After all, they are probably to be found growing as wild plants in natural grassland somewhere in the world. They might be able to compete with the grass and flourish, or they might not. Those most likely to succeed are those with a dense clump of basal leaves, which will shade out the grass immediately around themselves.

Planting using nursery-grown plants

Planting using conventional-sized nursery-grown plants is liable to be expensive for all but the smallest areas. It is also difficult to achieve this way the multilayered complexity of natural grassland habitats – although in a small space this might not matter too much. Specialist suppliers will advise on the spacing of plants – that is, the number to be fitted into a unit area. Planting is normally at random.

If the delicate grass *Briza minor* is growing, it is a sign that the soil is dry and low in nutrients – ideal conditions for colourful limestone grassland wildflowers.

85

Among the many species suitable for annual meadows are poppies and *Phacelia tanacetifolia* (above), *Linum grandiflorum* var. *rubrum* and *Eschscholzia californica* (below).

Planting using 'plugs' or 'cell trays'

Plugs are the small plants that are grown in potting compost in multicell plastic trays in wholesale nurseries. They are a very cost-effective way of growing large numbers of plants. You can easily obtain the trays second-hand from commercial nurseries, who often throw out vast numbers in the spring. Generally the larger sizes (around 2 cm/¾ inch wide) are the most useful. Seed can be sown directly into the trays, or, alternatively, it can be sown in conventional pots or seed trays and seedlings later transplanted into the trays.

Plants can be grown one per cell, to produce single-plant plugs; or seed mixtures, such as a meadow grass and wildflower mixture, can be sown instead, to create multiplant plugs. Once the plants have filled the cells with roots, they are ready for planting.

Because of the small size of plugs, the soil for planting needs to be well broken up and raked. Plugs can be speedily planted – using a dibber or a narrow trowel – around 15 cm/6 inches apart. Planting in rows makes hoeing off weeds between the plants easier.

Planting meadow wildflowers into existing grass

Existing grass – a lawn, perhaps – can be made into a meadow by adding wildflowers to it. However, this will work only if the soil is not highly fertile and the grass is of the very fine type, rather than one of the vigorous broader-leaved varieties, which would be too competitive for the successful establishment of the wildflowers. Circles of turf around 30 cm/12 inches wide can be cut out and wildflowers planted in the resulting hole. Alternatively, smaller pieces of turf can be removed, and plugs planted, at a spacing of 15–20 cm/6–8 inches. This can rapidly result in a good-looking meadow. Wildflowers or perennials with a dense clump-like habit, such as many geraniums, are the most likely to be successful.

In theory this approach could be used with prairie plants, but given that turf grasses are not natives of North America, and can out-compete many prairie plants, it is unlikely to be successful in the long term.

Sowing seed

Suppliers usually include plenty of detailed advice about seed-sowing in their literature, which should be followed closely.

Small-scale meadow sowing has the advantage that it is easier to keep a close eye on the planting as it develops. Weeding out unwanted aggressive species is the most important task, and sowing or planting in straight lines will certainly make this task easier, as they will be clearly visible as those plants not growing in rows.

Managing meadows

Being an extremely dynamic plant community, grassland responds well to management. Consider what happens if a wildflower-rich hay meadow is not mown. Last year's grass begins to build up, forming a thick thatch which after a couple of years impedes the growth of the less vigorous wildflowers. Meanwhile the strongest-growing grasses begin to form dense tussocks, and the growth of the slower-growing more delicate grass species gradually reduces. Over time, natural seeding results in the stronger grasses displacing other grasses and wildflowers, resulting in a loss of biodiversity. The finer grasses and wildflowers benefit from mowing because it reduces the competition of the less desirable grasses: removal of clippings has the effect of taking away the two key elements that stimulate plant growth, nitrogen and phosphorus, from which the 'greedy' fast-growing grasses benefit most. The progressive removal of the less desirable grasses shifts the balance towards the more desirable wildflowers.

Mowing then is essential, to encourage a wide range of species to flourish; it is particularly important for the first year or two after the establishment of new meadows and prairies, to help reduce the growth of the more vigorous constituents, especially the grasses, and allow slower-growing plants to catch up.

But when? Meadows are at their best in the early to mid-summer period. Since we want plants to regenerate naturally, it seems sensible to let them seed, which means waiting a while longer before mowing, perhaps until late summer. However, meadows often begin to look untidy by mid-summer, and this is particularly noticeable in a small garden. Cutting back after the first flush of flowering, before the plants set seed, will result in regrowth, and any later-summer-flowering species will still flower, albeit at a shorter height. Another mowing in autumn, after the plants have set seed, will tidy up the meadow for the winter, although ideally this should be delayed as long as possible to allow wildlife to feed from old seed heads. In mild winter climates, another end-of-winter mow may be necessary, but it is important to do this before any bulbs start to emerge.

A prairie with *Rudbeckia fulgida* in the foreground and *Ratibida pinnata*, with reflexed yellow petals, further back. *R. pinnata* performs well on heavy clay soils.

Established for over twenty years, this meadow planting around a suburban house is now very species-rich, because nutrient levels have fallen over the years as grass clippings have been removed. The sward includes *Rhinanthus minor*, a semi-parasite on grass, which by weakening the grass enables more wildflowers to flourish.

A meadow whose wildflowers are all early-summer-flowering, with species such as ox-eye daisy (*Leucanthemum vulgare*) and harebell (*Campanula rotundifolia*), can be mown once the main flowering is over, preferably after they've set seed, and kept mown, at about 5 cm / 2 inches high, for the rest of the summer. The texture of the lawn will be coarser than is normal because of the presence of the wildflowers.

FLOWERING LAWNS

Many gardeners will be glad to know that there is a halfway house between the lawn and the meadow. The spring 'mini-meadow' or flowering lawn makes use of the fact that early-flowering meadow plants and bulbs are short – much shorter than later-flowering ones (which is logical, as the latter have a longer time in which to grow). Many bulbs, particularly crocuses and narcissi, are commonly grown in grass anyway, and since the grass should not be cut before their foliage has yellowed in early summer, many gardeners are stuck with an area of gradually growing grass until then. It makes sense to have something attractive growing in the grass whilst it is there.

Certain wildflowers often end up introducing themselves into grass in any case; daisies (*Bellis perennis*) are well known as lawn 'weeds' and are often joined by other 'weeds', such as self-heal (*Prunella vulgaris*). By introducing plants into the turf, or by sowing wildflower seed with the grass seed when the lawn in sown, it is possible to add other wildflowers, such as cowslips (*Primula veris*) and lady's smock

(*Cardamine pratensis*). The result will be a short (10–20 cm/4–8 inches) turf spangled with wildflowers. By the time the grass is cut in early summer, at least some of these should have set seed. From then on, the grass can be cut regularly, and the area maintained as a conventional, albeit rather rough-textured, lawn.

A basic mini-meadow can often be established with minimum effort, simply by not mowing until early summer, and allowing daisies and any other species that join them to spread naturally. It can be an interesting exercise to let nature take its own course and see what happens.

PRAIRIES

Prairies are the opposite of meadows, as they are a plant community of deep fertile soils. Originally restricted to the mid-western states of North America, prairie-type vegetation can now also be seen in many other areas of eastern North America, where human intervention has destroyed the old forest cover. Prairie wildflowers are numerous and very beautiful – indeed many have ended up as popular garden plants. Because they rely on rich soils, they are also big: prairies in late autumn can be more than head height.

Because of its height, prairie vegetation is difficult to fit into the very smallest spaces without it looking out of place. However, since most prairie species are late-summer or autumn-flowering, a prairie-style planting can be cut back to within 10 cm/4 inches of the base of the plants in early summer and then allowed to regrow, to flower at a much shorter height, generally under 1 metre/3½ feet. Such mini-prairies can be highly effective.

European gardeners on fertile soils are beginning to look towards prairie wildflowers as an alternative to native meadow wildflowers in urban areas. Their late flowering season means that they are a boon for butterflies.

Prairies can be created by sowing or by planting nursery-grown plants, as for meadows – see above.

Selecting species

As with meadows, commercially available prairie seed mixes for different soil types are recommended. It is important to get the right mix, as species that flourish on clay may not do so on sand, and vice versa. The species composition of the seed mixes, which is usually given in the seed catalogue, can also be used as a

BEE ROOSTING PLACES

Many 'solitary' bees – that is, those that don't form hives – run short of places to roost and nest in tidy gardens. You can give them, and other insects, a helping hand by making stacks of short lengths of bamboo canes, into which they can slip themselves for shelter, nesting or hibernating. The most convenient way to do this is to pile them up into a frame, which holds them tight. You can then attach the frame to a wall or post in a sheltered spot.

guide to the plants that should be chosen if you are going to plant a mini-prairie rather than use seed. Some nurseries sell collections of plants for planting small prairies.

If you are making your own selection of prairie plants for a small garden, it is possible to use a higher proportion of forbs to grasses than would be the case for a 'full-size' planting, which will make the mini-prairie more decorative. Since there is a wide range of species available, it should be possible to make a selection on the basis of peak flowering season, height and colour.

Managing prairies

Fire, which maintains prairie naturally, is also the most effective management tool. However, burning is often impractical or dangerous on a small scale; mowing is an alternative. Burning in mid-spring before the prairie plants have started to grow kills unwanted weedy grasses and limits the growth of the more aggressive prairie wildflowers, such as goldenrods. Mowing will have a similar effect, but a less marked one, which means that if weedy invaders are a problem, additional measures to control them will be necessary. After cutting down the dead remains of last season's growth, you can mow the remaining stems and weeds, which will knock back the undesirables. You can then treat the ground with a flame-gun to simulate the effects of burning.

While burning last year's growth keeps minerals in circulation, cutting and removing the dead growth takes minerals out of the prairie system. Composting the dead material and returning it the following winter is a possible way of stopping the progressive impoverishment of the soil. Alternatively you can feed it into a shredder and spread the shredded material over the garden as mulch. If you use a strimmer or weed-eater, you can shred the prairie plants *in situ* as they are cut down.

ABOVE A boardwalk is a good vantage point from which to appreciate a garden prairie. This example is in the north of England. Although the plants are not native, they still provide food for a wide variety of insects.

OPPOSITE The pink *Echinacea purpurea* is a popular prairie plant. It is relatively short-lived, however, so eventually it is displaced by other species. Prairies such as this flourish on fertile soils in regions with cold winters and hot summers. Gardeners are now exploring the possibilities of prairies for regions with a less severe climate.

Wetlands are some of the most exciting of all natural habitats, buzzing with life – insects, birds and plants. Yet the human race has always been ambivalent about them; being difficult to traverse or exploit, they have often been seen as threatening or undesirable. Partly because of this fact, they have been destroyed on a huge scale – which makes it all the more important that we do something to redress this loss. And we can: in the garden even the tiniest pool can be an oasis for wildlife, an opportunity for observing a rich ecosystem in miniature.

Although this pool is edged with a hard material, the gradient is sufficiently low to allow animals to reach the water to drink, and amphibians to climb out. The vegetation on one side provides cover.

WETLANDS

Wetlands are the most productive natural environments, the constant supply of water making lush growth possible over a long season. This productivity is reflected in the wealth of wildlife that live in them – something that can be appreciated within a matter of hours after the creation of a new garden pond, as birds home in to drink and water-dwelling insects appear. The wonder of a garden pond is that there is so much animal life as well as plantlife to be appreciated, and therefore the opportunity to see whole ecosystems in action. An associated wetland area is also an opportunity to grow a luxuriant array of plants.

While formal pools generally offer only open water with a hard edge or surround, the essence of a natural pond is the presence of a gradient from open water to dry land. Every stage in the transition has different flora and indeed fauna. Taking a natural pond as a model offers all sorts of possibilities to the gardener, who could fit into a small space a variety of different plant species with very different forms, which will make an attractive haven for wildlife.

A wetland area associated with a pond adds yet another dimension to a garden. It makes it possible to grow the kind of lush waterside vegetation that never looks its best when grown in ordinary garden soil. It also extends the wildlife-friendly environment of the pond, providing a place where a variety of creatures can approach the water under cover. A wetland also creates a context for a pond. Formal pools are one thing, an artificial creation whose intention is obvious, but an informal pool surrounded by grass or other obviously dry-land vegetation can look isolated and out of place. In nature pools are always surrounded by wet areas that support plant communities with distinctive species, such as reeds or rushes.

Wetland and waterside vegetation is distinctive because of its relationship to the abundance of water. Plentiful water, along with the often high concentration of nutrients in wetland areas, allows for unrestricted growth. Not surprisingly, plants grow large and lush – indeed they have to, as any that don't establish elbow room will be smothered by their neighbours. Because of this, flowering is usually delayed; the plant does not put energy into reproduction until it has firmly established its presence. Many wetland plants do not flower until mid-summer, and there are relatively (almost frustratingly) few early-flowering species. Wetland plants tend to be big – which is a problem for us, as large plants will soon

ABOVE Rodgersia, with its panicles of creamy flowers, and glossy-leaved lysichiton flourish at the water's edge. A colourful sculpture provides a focus.

OPPOSITE A narrow planted strip between water and paving gives a more naturalistic feeling than a hard surface abutting straight on to the water.

overwhelm a small garden pond or wetland, physically as well as visually. Finding small-growing species is a key part of making a successful small-scale wetland.

Roots immersed in water, or in waterlogged soils, cannot breathe. With most plants, this can result in root death or attack by fungus diseases. Wetland plants have a variety of physiological means of overcoming this problem, which enable them to survive in situations where other plants cannot, but many do not need wet soil to survive, and will grow perfectly well in ordinary garden soil. However, there are also some plants which, though often described as 'moisture-loving', are not at all tolerant of waterlogging. By nature they are plants of seasonally wet habitats, or places where water flows through the soil but without excluding air, such as streamsides. The bronze-leaved rodgersias are an example. Put them in a wetland area or bog garden, where there is no air in the water, and they will die. Unfortunately, reference books are not always very clear about this distinction. When choosing plants it is advisable to seek the advice of specialist nurserymen, who grow all their own plants, and thus know them and their needs intimately.

PLANNING A POND

Ponds are rightly popular as garden features. They have enormous power to act as a visual focus, and consequently tend to become the centre of attention as soon as they come into view. This means that in a small garden they will often dominate. When designing a small garden, it is important to bear this in mind and make the pond an integral, if not a key, part of the whole design.

A pond fulfils a number of possibly contradictory purposes in the garden: as a focus for our enjoyment, as part of an overall design involving planting, and as a wildlife resource. The first purpose often means that there is a sitting place next to the pond, which makes a vantage point from which to view wildlife, but of course some wildlife prefers privacy. The solution is to ensure that the pond has two clear zones: a human end and a wild end. The former can have a clear-cut edge, of paving or decking, perhaps as part of a larger sitting-out area with a table and chairs; the latter can have a habitat gradient and a gentle slope down to the water. It makes sense to have the wild end backing on to other wild areas of the garden.

Natural ponds are always an irregular shape, and in many garden situations this fits into the feel of the garden. In small and urban gardens, this may not be the case; a pond that is trying to look natural in an environment where one would not

OPPOSITE
Top left: Even the tiniest pond will support wildlife if it has boggy margins where a few marshland plants can grow.
Top right: Large plants such as the huge-leaved *Petasites japonicus* seen here can work well in small gardens, creating a dramatic effect; they may become invasive, however, if their growth is not restricted.
Bottom left: Candelabra primulas are among the liveliest waterside plants, often self-seeding liberally. Here, in early summer, they flower next to *Alchemilla mollis*.
Bottom right: Bog gardens allow a wide range of lush wetland plants to thrive, but may need topping up in dry periods.

Boardwalks and decking combine well with water, and provide access points that are less environmentally disruptive than paving, as they allow wildlife to get underneath. Suspended above water, they make a vantage point from which it is possible to see what is happening even in relatively deep waters.

expect to find a natural pond will perhaps not succeed in the illusion. 'Formal' pools, with their straight edges and geometry, are not meant to look natural but as we have seen usually have hard edges and so are unsympathetic to wildlife or to much marginal vegetation. But why not combine the two? A 'canal' shape – that is, long and narrow – is a good way of achieving this. My garden features a pond of this shape. It has a sitting area at one end but the two long sides merge with strips of bog garden running alongside. The water surface is thus seen as a rectangle almost completely surrounded by lush wetland vegetation.

Ponds are generally positioned so that they receive sun. It is a good idea to have some shade too, so that fish and other water creatures can shelter during hot weather. There is no reason why a garden pond should not be in light shade, as there are plenty of waterside plants that will thrive. However, if the shade is supplied by trees, there will be an annual autumnal task of dredging out fallen leaves.

WETLAND AREAS IN THE GARDEN

A garden wetland, or bog garden, with or without an adjoining pond, provides an opportunity to grow a wide and exciting range of plants. Characteristic of much wetland vegetation are large leaf sizes and an overall luxuriant appearance. Where a garden wetland is providing naturalistic context for a pond, getting the vegetation right is important if onlookers are to 'read' your efforts as being natural.

In nature the gradient from water to dry land is often complex, because there is a succession of habitats from open water to dry land. Many open water bodies get progressively shallower as streams flowing into them pour in silt, and as they do so it becomes easier for marginal vegetation to creep in from the sides – chiefly large grasses such as reeds – and the open water becomes a marsh. As the grasses lay down more and more dead leaves and stems, the ground level builds up, and provides an environment where certain tree and shrub seedlings can take root, such as species of alder and willow. These progressively dry out the ground and

cause the soil to build up. The end result is conditions that favour locally dominant tree species, which start to grow and begin to form a stable forest community.

Visually, this succession gradient has several key elements, which will be familiar, and often evocative, to anybody who has explored such environments in the wild. One is the fringe of reeds (or similar large grasses) that surrounds many a pond or lake. Another is the loose scrub that forms in the drier parts of the marshland – places that are often almost impossible to pass through, a tangled mass of branches, trunks, reeds and small pools of open water. Garden planting should evoke the different ingredients of this environment, which can be conjured up with just a few strategic elements around a pond, such as grasses or rushes in a wetland area by the pond edge, and one or two appropriate coppiced shrubs.

The best ponds have a gradient which offers a variety of stages and conditions between open water and dry land. Here white *Iris ensata* stands at the water's edge, while yellow candelabra primula hybrids, along with a white arum lily (*Zantedeschia aethiopica*), relish the constant moisture at the edge of the 'dry land'.

The kingcup (*Caltha palustris*) is one of the earliest waterside plants to flower in spring. The wood piles here should provide cover for a variety of invertebrates.

MAKING PONDS AND WETLANDS

Details of how to make ponds can be found in specialist books on water gardening. Essentially, construction involves using a strong rubber or plastic liner to hold water. Safety is an important concern, especially if there are children around. It may be sensible to build a raised edge, and it is possible to get nets that are designed to lie just under the water surface to catch any child who might fall in.

In our case we want to ensure that we have opportunities for the development of a gradient where marginal plants can thrive. Depending upon the pond size, it is a good idea to have a variety of depths, as many plants will only grow successfully at the right depth. A maximum depth of at least 50 cm/20 inches ensures that there are areas of water that stay cool in hot weather, essential for many pond dwellers. Shelves along the side of the pool allow for marginal plants to be sited, growing either in pots with holes in the side, or in soil laid on the shelves. Extending the shelves sideways makes a strip for a bog garden on the side. This way, the wetland area is an integral part of the pond. However, during dry weather it will soak up water from the pond, accelerating the rate at which the pond water level drops, and regular refilling will be necessary.

A wetland area can be made quite independently of a pond, simply by lining a hollow with a pond liner and backfilling with soil. The soil layer should be at least 30 cm/12 inches deep, and the edge of the plastic concealed. The resulting bog garden will need watering during dry weather, and you should take great care to use garden tools very carefully in the vicinity in order to avoid piercing the liner.

Even if there is no possibility of creating a true wetland, perhaps because there is an already existing hard-edged pond, it is still possible to create a planting by the side of a pond which features species that look like genuine wetland plants. And these will also perform the important function of providing cover for wildlife to approach the water. As already pointed out, some wetland plants, many irises for example, are perfectly happy to grow in ordinary garden conditions. Among the species that can be used to evoke wetland, the miscanthus grasses are invaluable, as they are very adaptable and look like an elegant version of the common reed.

Very small gardens, or gardens without any soil, can have ponds and wetlands too. A variety of containers, including recycled industrial containers, can be used to hold water. Since the size of such containers is limited, it will only be possible to create a mini-pond or a small-scale wetland, and the usefulness to wildlife of such container water and bog gardens will be seriously reduced, compared to even the smallest 'proper' garden pond, because of difficulties of access. Nevertheless, they can still be an attractive and interesting feature.

SELECTING WATER AND WETLAND PLANTS

Since it is in the very nature of water and wetland plants to grow large – they almost have to, in order to compete in a resource-rich environment – many a small garden pond rapidly becomes overwhelmed with plants that choke it or completely cover it. Despite the relative shortage of small-growing plants, there are some miniature water and wetland plants, which are often small-growing forms of other species, and if you can seek these out from specialist nurseries you will save yourself a lot of trouble. It is fortunate that there are some good miniature water lilies, some of which only need 30 cm/12 inches of water.

It is more important, though, from an ecological point of view, to select non-invasive species. This is because some water plants, introduced to regions where they are not native, have run amok, and choked streams and ponds, smothering native species. This has usually happened because people have foolishly disposed of surplus plants in waterways, but it is possible that birds can distribute plants through material carried on their feet. Many countries or states now have lists of plant species that are known to cause problems and should be avoided.

BOGS FOR ACID SOILS

Although the term 'bog garden' is commonly used to describe any area kept wet for moisture-loving plants, 'bog' (or 'peat bog') has a very specific meaning for ecologists. It describes wetlands where water and soil have a very low nutrient content and a high acidity. These are unfavourable for the growth of most wetland plants. Consequently these areas, or acid bogs, and the wetter areas of pine barrens (a term used in the US for a habitat that is similar to moorland and heathland – see page 108) have their own distinctive flora, including plants that have evolved to eat insects, to make up for the lack of nitrogen and phosphorus in the soil.

STONES FOR INVERTEBRATES AND AMPHIBIANS

Large flat stones can be a very good habitat for a wide variety of insects, woodlice and other invertebrates. This food supply, plus the cool damp conditions, attracts amphibians such as newts and some smaller reptiles. These animals will forage more widely at night and can play an important role in eating pests throughout the garden.

ABOVE By deliberately planting an area as wetland you can make the most of damp or occasionally waterlogged areas in the garden.

OPPOSITE Peat bogs are home to specialized flora, of which insectivorous plants, such as these *Sarracenia* species, with their pitcher-like leaf stalks, are the most extraordinary.

As the low level of nutrients does not encourage much growth, these plants tend to be much smaller than wetland plants from high-nutrient-level areas. There can be a considerable number of species growing around the tiniest pool, with small variations in water level enabling the growth of different plant species, all producing a feeling of a world in miniature.

Bogs are very dependent upon soil and water chemistry and are only likely to succeed in areas where both are naturally acidic. You can easily see if your garden is suitable by using a soil test kit. Pond liner can be used to create a bog area if the soil is not naturally wet. Bog soils are naturally high in undecomposed organic matter – peat – and in a garden a bog should aim to copy this. Peat digging, of course, can be immensely destructive to natural boglands, and it would seem a sad irony to use the spoils of the destruction of natural bogs in order to create artificial ones. However, there are some brands of peat available which do not involve this destructive 'mining'. Alternatives to peat should be organic in origin and acidic. Shredded dry bracken and conifer needles or conifer leaf mould are suitable, and often easily available.

Many bog plants are commercially available; nurseries specializing in alpines and rockery plants are often a good source. Regions where pine barrens or other acid soils are extensive may have nurseries specializing in this type of flora. There are also specialist insectivorous plant growers. The moss and sedge flora that is so distinctive and important a part of the vegetation may not be so easy to buy. Sometimes they can be 'rescued' from sites where construction work threatens existing flora. If you do this, you should seek the agreement of landowners first.

Mosses such as bog mosses (*Sphagnum* spp.) and hair mosses (*Polystichum* spp.) are a vital part of bogs, responsible for a lot of the rich visual appeal of the habitat when seen close to. Small sedges (*Carex* spp.) and rushes (*Juncus* spp.) are an important matrix vegetation too. Dwarf shrubs such as *Ledum groenlandicum*, *Kalmia angustifolia* and various species of *Gaultheria* and *Vaccinium* play a showier role. Heathers, such as *Erica tetralix*, can also play a part. These low shrubby plants play a more dominant role on hummocks, which do not get so wet – in fact they are the next stage in the succession process.

Insectivorous plants provide a level of interest that is utterly different from that of any other habitat. Many are very beautiful as well, and all repay close attention. While only a few are completely frost hardy, the others can often be protected with conifer branches and bracken in the winter.

DRY AND EXPOSED HABITATS

Our attitude to places exposed to the elements is full of contradictions. They are powerfully linked in the imagination to the supposed unkindness of nature, such as the 'blasted heath' where the winds howl and the witches gather. Yet many of us happily hike in or otherwise enjoy their open spaces and long views. And it is a paradox that extreme conditions have led plants to evolve in ways that we find both beautiful and very practical. The plants that grow in these often difficult conditions include some of the most popular and most frequently planted of all.

Plants of exposed places, such as the grass *Stipa tenuissima*, often have a spare beauty of their own. A perennial wallflower, *Erysimum* 'Bowles' Mauve', flowers behind the grass.

DRY AND EXPOSED HABITATS

ABOVE The coast is perhaps the most testing of all temperate plant habitats. Leathery low-growing species are the norm, with specially adapted trees such as this tamarisk (*Tamarix ramosissima*) which, like the blue *Perovskia atriplicifolia* in the foreground, comes from central Asia, bitterly cold in winter and hot in summer.

OPPOSITE Varieties of perennial wallflower *Erysimum* 'Bowles' Mauve' and lavender flower alongside the large green heads of *Euphorbia characias* subsp. *wulfenii*. All flourish in dry soils and make good gravel garden plants.

Wind-swept heathland and moorland, sun-baked dry scrub, the seaside – at first glance these are all rather different habitats. But they share certain characteristics: even particular groups of plants reappear in what may seem very different places. The common factor is that in all of these environments plants are vulnerable to water loss. While this is perhaps obvious in areas with a Mediterranean climate, or by the coast, it is less clear why this should be so in higher-latitude or higher-altitude moorland. But here too winds of high velocity strip soft plant growth of moisture, so plants can become dehydrated very quickly. This problem is exacerbated by the thin stony soils that are often found in these places: these have limited reserves of ground water for roots to draw on, and tend to have low levels of nutrients.

A cursory look at plants from all these different habitats soon reveals a great many similarities: the flora from each includes small, often dwarf, shrubs with a tight branching pattern and masses of tiny leaves; narrow-leaved tough grasses; and very small herbaceous plants that shelter in the lee of others. The superficial similarity in foliage and form of (moorland) heathers, (Mediterranean) wild herbs like thymes and lavenders and (New Zealand) hebes is not just coincidental. In many cases these are adaptations to environments where water loss is a major limitation on plant growth.

Plants have evolved to survive in these rather hostile environments by minimizing their vulnerability to water loss and to the factors that lead to it. Reduced leaf size makes plants less exposed to both the sun and strong or dry winds. Tough evergreen leaves conserve resources, whilst coatings of wax or hair protect leaves against sun, wind and ultra-violet light. Plants of hot, dry environments commonly have a silver or grey appearance, resulting from a covering of tiny hairs on the surface of leaves and stems. Oils and gums reduce water loss, so many are aromatic. Spines or very tough leaves are frequent, to ward off hungry animals – an additional risk factor in places where limited resources make all growth 'expensive' for a plant; wax and hair

Heathers are the quintessential acid-soil plants, also well able to cope with exposure and difficult soils. The winter-flowering *Erica carnea*, seen here with snowdrops (*Galanthus* 'Atkinsii'), is almost unique in that it will grow on alkaline as well as acid soils.

also make leaves less palatable to wildlife. The tight branching and small leaves which help to reduce exposure to sun and wind and consequent desiccation also give these plants an attractive appearance. Their visual qualities and powers of survival combine to assure for them a place in our gardens.

So heathland and moorland, hot, dry areas and coastal sites – which at first seem very different places – share characteristics which have caused the plants that grow in them to adapt in similar ways. However, the gardener wishing to cope with a challenging site, or even just to create visually pleasing and natural-looking plantings, needs to understand the finer details of each of these environments.

MOORLAND, HEATHLAND AND PINE BARRENS

Two factors make life difficult for plants in areas of moor and heath: acid soils and strong winds. The two are often linked – historic deforestation had led to increased exposure, which together with the acidity of the soil reduces the rate of new tree growth. Dwarf shrubs, many belonging to the heather and rhododendron family (the *Ericaceae*) dominate in these areas, often forming a tangled mat of vegetation. Grasses, sedges and rushes can play an important part ecologically and visually, along with a limited number of herbaceous perennials. In wetter areas, bog plants, including many insectivorous species, take over (see page 101).

The remarkable thing for us as gardeners is how the unfavourable conditions have encouraged the evolution of plants whose protective characteristics have made them useful ornamentals. Heathers and hebes (the latter from montane New Zealand habitats) are some of the best-selling ornamental shrubs. Their neat habit and attractive, often coloured, evergreen foliage looks good for twelve months of the year. And their tight, ground-hugging habit gives them a practical advantage, for it makes them excellent weed-suppressors. The spectacular flowering of many, heathers especially, is an added bonus. With all these qualities, no wonder that they are planted in their millions – to the extent that they have become almost horticultural clichés – in places that little resemble their natural habitats.

Pine barrens is a habitat that is similar to moorland and heathland but often less afflicted by wind, and usually with more forest cover. It too is dominated by a very specialized plant community, which includes both small-growing shrubs and perennials, some of which have considerable ornamental potential.

Selecting plants

The possibilities of these habitats as inspiration for the small garden with acidic or very sandy soil are obvious: compact plant species that naturally have a strong tendency to intermesh seem to provide a perfect recipe for a naturalistic planting combination. This intermeshed evergreen foliage is an excellent ground cover, effectively suppressing weed growth – so making it one of the best low-maintenance planting styles. However, in many gardens this has resulted in an artificial 'heathers and conifers' look. So, how to combine these plants in a naturalistic and creative way?

Grasses, and especially sedges (Carex spp.), are natural companions for heathers. They provide an effective contrast in form, texture and often colour.

Modelling a planting on a local habitat is an obvious way to proceed, using locally common native species as a basis or matrix, and including other more decorative species for their ornamental effect. These habitats often have a very distinctive 'look' about them, resulting from the combination of particular elements: a matrix of dwarf wiry shrubs, grasses with a distinct habit or colour and localized taller shrubs such as upright junipers or bushy, almost contorted pines. Some of the most useful plants for this habitat are New Zealand sedges such as *Carex testacea* or *C. comans* with russet or bronze-coloured foliage. There are a lot of cultivars of some plants, heathers especially, which have bright, very unnatural-looking colours. Avoid these, along with those that have highly coloured flowers. Use 'dwarf' conifers very sparingly, especially those with golden foliage, as they are largely responsible for the banal appearance of many examples of this kind of planting.

A heathland-type planting that is not so closely modelled on a natural environment is an opportunity to combine a wide range of dwarf shrubs, including the reliable and colourful heathers (*Calluna, Daboecia* and *Erica* spp.), the very similar, but perhaps less easy *Phyllodoce* and *Cassiope* genera, and their very different-looking

close relatives, *Vaccinium* (including the commercial cranberry and blueberry) and *Gaultheria*. These have small broad leaves, often with an attractive bronze flush when young, clusters of tiny white flowers and quite showy berries. Dwarf rhododendrons can be included too. Part of the joy of these plants is the way that they tend to run into each other, forming a tight mat of vegetation whose texture and rich variety of leaf shapes and colours is a year-round pleasure. Grasses make a striking contrast.

While the foliage interest of acidic-soil plants is strong for twelve months of the year, flowering can be spectacular, with most species flowering in spring or early summer, but with certain heathers flowering in mid- or late summer, or even in late winter. Autumn berrries can be a feature too.

THIN, DRY SOILS

Gardening on a dry soil in an area with hot, dry summers and cold winters may seem a thankless task. You may not even be in a severe-climate zone; trying to get plants to grow in a bed along the foundations of a house in thin soil in a sunny position can be very unrewarding too. Even very sandy soils can cause problems for many common garden plants. Many of the drought-resistant plants that are recommended for such dry sites are from Mediterranean-climate zones, and may not be hardy. Yet there are other species that are more suitable for such sites; and 'semi-desert' areas — whether they are confined to a small site or derive from the climatic character of a region — can be very rewarding if planted appropriately. The small size of many of the species that will thrive is an advantage, making it possible to plant up even narrow strips with dwarf bulbs, smaller-growing evergreen grasses and colourful wildflowers.

There are various natural habitats that are dominated by grasses but which are very different from meadow environments, because of severe summer drought. Rather than forming a dense sod, as in meadow or prairie, the grasses in these habitats are much thinner, and more clearly visible as individual clumps. In such areas there is often a much wider range than there is in meadows of non-grassy plants, such as herbaceous perennials, small shrubs and, in some regions, 'spiky' rosette plants such as yuccas; very often a dramatic display of spring bulbs too. The short-grass prairie of North America, forming a bridge between the lush tall-grass prairie and the true arid zone, is a good example; the steppe of eastern Europe and western Asia is another. Both may seem inhospitable at first, but as in many

ABOVE The grey leaves of mulleins (*Verbascum* spp.) and the narrow leaves of the grass *Stipa tenuissima* are characteristic of dry habitats. A gravel garden allows the mulleins to self-sow and develop a relaxed and spontaneous appearance.

OPPOSITE Gravel gardens provide a good context for a variety of drought-resistant plants, such as these grasses and *Eryngium* species. Although they look like thistles, eryngiums are umbellifers (members of the cow parsley family).

The grass *Stipa tenuissima* and 'everlasting' *Anaphalis triplinervis* make an effective mid-summer combination in this steppe planting.

seasonally dry places their wildflowers put on a spectacular display of early colour, and there may be high levels of diversity. Plants flower and seed before there is a danger of summer drought, so their season is brief but showy, and they try to conserve resources by having evergreen leaves, rather than waste precious moisture and nutrients by having leaves that last for only a few months. With protective grey or silver wax or hair layers on many of them, the leaves are attractive all year round – which gives these plants quite an advantage over plants from lusher environments.

Particularly important in many arid areas are a group of plants sometimes called 'sagebrush', almost midway in character between shrubs and herbaceous perennials. Highly aromatic and grey-leaved, they include many artemisias and the highly ornamental (and usefully mid-summer-flowering) perovskia. Some of the more attractive ones are already well established as garden plants.

There is often quite an overlap in species between related habitats: many European dry limestone wildflowers appear in steppes too, for example, and a few Mediterranean species. But the difference between them and Mediterranean climates is the winter cold, which can often be very intense – too cold for many of the drought-tolerant shrubs typical of Mediterranean environments. Likewise some tall-grass prairie plants, such as the spectacular orange *Asclepias tuberosa*, recur in the short-grass regions, because of their relative drought-tolerance.

Selecting plants

Key to the look of many 'semi-desert' areas are grasses, especially those with a distinct clump-forming habit, grey or blue foliage (for example, *Helictotrichon sempervirens*) or distinct flower heads (for example, many *Stipa* spp.). For the small garden or narrow strip border, the grass *S. tenuissima* is invaluable, with its long season of delicate seed heads, and it is small enough to use as multiples in quite a small space, successfully evoking a meadow in even 1 square metre/3½ square feet. It is also a splendid visual foil for the colours and textures of flowers and broader-leaved plants. It is short-lived but readily self-sows.

Many perennials from dry meadow habitats will flourish in this kind of situation, such as the various blue and purple cultivars of *Salvia nemorosa*, along with many species of poppy and iris, such as *Iris unguicularis*, which always seems happiest growing in builder's rubble.

Sagebrush plants are an important element for a naturalistic look, and their long season of grey foliage can play a vital visual role. However, they all tend to be scruffy in habit, many developing particularly untidy rangy stems. If this happens, do not be afraid to cut them hard back to ground level every winter.

Dry meadow environments are often rich in bulbs, which pop up quickly in the brief spring, flower and then retreat underground for the worst of the hot summer. There are a host of dwarf tulip species from central Asia, while North America has *Calochortus* and *Fritillaria*. More dramatic are the foxtail lilies (*Eremurus* spp.), with their statuesque spikes packed with thousands of flowers. Those gardening on 'normal' soils find them difficult to grow, but they love semi-desert conditions. A good summer 'baking' is vital for nearly all these bulbs, which means that in cooler climes they should not be shaded by other plants.

Annuals often thrive in 'cold desert' environments, especially if the soil is thin and sandy (which makes it easy for seedlings to germinate) and the vegetation is sparse. In the garden this means that hardy annuals – of which there is a wide range – can be a rewarding addition to a border dominated by perennials.

Of all habitats, that of thin dry soil is perhaps the one where the least amount of plant selection has been carried out by the nursery industry. It does not help that dry grassland environments are not great holiday destinations! Those who live in or visit such regions can always collect seed of locally abundant species and be horticultural pioneers, trying out potentially newly cultivated plants in their gardens. Otherwise there is perhaps scope in using many of the species sold as 'rockery' or 'alpine' plants. These are nearly all compact, and many are cold- and drought-resistant, and repay more experimentation in 'non-rockery' conditions.

HOT, DRY 'MEDITERRANEAN' HABITATS

A Mediterranean climate has cool, wet winters and hot, dry summers. Outside the Mediterranean climate zones, in hot, dry situations in the garden – particularly in inner-city locations where temperature ranges are often much higher than is

Sempervivums are one of the most drought-tolerant groups of temperate-zone plants. In this garden they are imaginatively combined in the centre of a more conventional garden setting.

A low ground-hugging habit and evergreen foliage are typical of many drought-tolerant plants.

'normal' for the region – many Mediterranean plants can be grown, provided the soil is well drained and minimum winter temperatures do not regularly fall below –10°C/14°F.

Much Mediterranean vegetation consists of low-growing, compact evergreen shrubs, often with grey, silver or glossy foliage. Many have aromatic oils in their leaves and historically have been used as herbs. This is a very attractive flora, and a very functional one for the gardener, a low evergreen habit making plants highly effective as weed-smotherers. Our model here is the maquis, the low scrub that is often to be found around the Mediterranean sea, where low-growing shrubs form a dense intertwined mat. For our purposes, though, we need to be careful about choosing species that are not going to take up too much space – common sage (*Salvia officinalis*), for example, can cover 1 square metre/3½ square feet in a couple of years.

Larger shrubs and trees play an important role in many Mediterranean-climate areas, and some have become positively iconic – as, for instance, the pencil-thin Italian cypresses (*Cupressus sempervirens)* and the olive (*Olea europaea*) throughout the Mediterranean region, or the madrones and manzanitas of California (*Arbutus menziesii* and *Arctostaphylos* spp. respectively). Since these trees do not cast a heavy shade and grow into wonderfully sculptural forms, there may well be room for one in even quite a small garden.

Annuals play a role in some Mediterranean climates – indeed the weeds of traditional cornfields, such as the field poppy (*Papaver rhoeas*) are originally from the eastern Mediterranean, as are several favourite cottage-garden annuals, including love-in-a-mist (*Nigella damascena*). Other Mediterranean-type climates have also contributed to our gardens, with plants such as the California poppy (*Eschscholzia californica*).

Bulbs are pre-eminently Mediterranean-climate plants and their lifestyle of winter or spring flowering and summer dormancy is ideally adapted for the short growing season characteristic of regions with hot dry summer climates. Tulips, grape hyacinths (*Muscari* spp.), freesias and many other bulbs, all from Mediterranean climates, have a potentially important part to play in the garden.

Selecting and using plants

A large part of planting a Mediterranean-climate-inspired garden is about evoking a sense of place – perhaps Italy, or Spain, or California. Given the importance of particular distinctive plant species in creating an ambience that everyone recognizes, choosing a few key plants is essential when designing such a garden.

Many Mediterranean-climate shrubs have a considerable history of cultivation, which means that there are a lot of species available, which is just as well, as shrubs play an important role in Mediterranean climates. Many grow too large for small gardens, which is potentially a limiting factor in what can be achieved in design terms. Some genera simply do not have any compact cultivars available – ceanothus, for example. It might be possible to keep one or two large cultivars contained, as suggested on page 73, but the extensive clipping that traditional gardeners often practise rather goes against the ethos of naturalistic gardening. Fortunately, however, there are some dwarf or compact-growing varieties available – cistus and the lavenders, for example, have an increasing number.

The lower maquis-type shrubs can be very useful, at least those that do not spread too much, including lavenders, sages (*Salvia* spp.), phlomis, teucrium and the showy halimium. These plants are particularly useful for hot dry banks, where they can be allowed to form a dense intertwined mat of evergreen, grey-toned foliage.

A distinctive part of the nature of Mediterranean vegetation that the gardener must take note of is the contribution that very different types of plant make to an overall decorative effect. Shrubs, nearly all evergreen, are the dominant element in terms of both time and space, their mostly grey or silver-toned foliage an attractive constant. Although some, such as the lavenders, are very decorative in flower, it is more ephemeral groups of plants that we depend upon for the main visual impact: bulbs and annuals. Mediterranean-climate herbaceous perennials tend to be small and do not play a large part in the big picture, but can be important for seasonal splashes of colour. While the selection available is not extensive, there are many that are very suitable for the smaller garden: among these are penstemons, many poppies, some irises and several of the small-growing

Blue or grey foliage is another distinctive feature of dry-zone plants. The characteristic colour is caused by a layer of either microscopic hairs or wax on the leaf surface; both serve to reduce water loss.

species of plants such as *Dianthus* and *Helianthemum,* often to be found in the 'rockery' section of the garden centre. Many grey- or silver-leaved grasses thrive in these conditions too, and their foliage shape contrasts well with that of the low shrubs. Some, such as species of *Stipa*, also have dramatic or beautiful seed heads.

As with other dry habitats, spring and early summer in Mediterranean-climate areas are a very colourful time, but there is relatively little flowering in the hot mid-summer period. In true Mediterranean areas there is often a 'second spring' in autumn, when many species choose to flower or repeat flower, often continuing well into winter. Both these flowering times are dominated by bulbs, of which a great variety can be fitted into a small space. Annuals are important too; these can be a very quick and easy source of colour. In true Mediterranean areas, most annuals are sown in the ground in the autumn, to flower in early to mid-summer, while in higher-latitude and cooler gardens, they are sown in spring, to flower from mid-summer into autumn. Annuals can be mixed in with shrubs and perennials but are most effective grown as a 'meadow' (see page 132).

Bulbs and annuals have had a long history of cultivation, which has included much selection and hybridization. Many of the resulting plants have lost the proportions, and indeed the colours, of their wild ancestors, tulips and marigolds (*Calendula* and *Tagetes* spp.) being obvious examples. Such 'unnatural' plants have their place, but perhaps not in the garden that aims to evoke nature and wildness.

Given the wide variety of plant form and colour available, the planting design of a Mediterranean garden offers a great deal of artistic scope. Low hummock forms can be contrasted with taller grassy and perennial ones; different leaf shapes can be set off against each other. So too can different leaf colours, while the predominant grey/silver foliage is an excellent foil for flower colours. The spiky form of Mediterranean perennials such as eryngium and acanthus can be particularly effective. Rosette-forming species such as yucca and agave offer serious drama.

If you are using bulbs, annuals and smaller perennials, you need to allow plenty of gaps when planting shrubs; otherwise the smaller plants will be overwhelmed. Bulbs will not get the summer 'baking' they need once they have died back if the top of the soil above them is shaded by shrubs or larger perennials.

In non-Mediterranean regions, a fashionable way of using these types of plants is the 'gravel garden', where a variety of mostly low shrubs and perennials are grown through a mulch of gravel. This is covered in more detail on page 134.

THE COAST

Coastal environments combine a whole raft of problems for plants: strong desiccating winds, poor soils and exposure to strong sunlight and to salt, which may be carried far inland during storms. There are a wide variety of coastal environments, all of them challenging for plants: cliffs, salt marshes, sand dunes and coastal grasslands. For the gardener in such environments, there is enormous potential in the landscape and the quality of the light; strong horizontals are often predominant, along with clear light and the subtle tones of sand, stone and bleached wood. Climatically there can be advantages too, as the sea tends to moderate temperatures, resulting in fewer frosts than inland.

Maritime plants tend to be similar in many ways to plants of other environments where desiccation is a potential problem. Thick or tough evergreen leaves are frequent, often with a grey waxy coating which is particularly attractive, or a covering of fine hairs.

There are relatively few plants within each geographical region that are truly coastal, in that they grow by the sea and nowhere else. Many plants that grow well in coastal areas are species that also thrive in mountain areas, or inland dry areas. Many coastal areas also have a distinctive non-native flora which has established itself in the variety of specialized ecological niches available: an example is offered by the 'Hottentot figs' (*Carpobrotus edulis*) from South Africa which are now found on many rocky coasts far from their original home.

Coastal gardening has been given a boost by the late Derek Jarman's garden on the south coast of England. This minimalist but extremely beautiful garden, which has been extensively written up in books and magazines, has made many people aware of just how much can be made from so little. The very sculptural quality of the maritime environment is emphasized by the combination of plants with driftwood and other items recovered from the shoreline. As the garden is right on the front line, only the most stress-tolerant plants are able to survive. These are often those that have the most dramatic qualities, such as sea kale (*Crambe maritima*) and sea holly (*Eryngium maritimum*). One of the greatest achievements of Jarman's garden has been in encouraging gardeners to engage with the sea and the coast,

Red valerian (*Centranthus ruber*) is a perennial able to survive in situations with a minimum of soil and little moisture. The poppies here (*Papaver commutatum*) are short-lived annuals which survive difficult dry periods as seed rather than living plants.

rather than trying, as gardeners have traditionally done, to seek protection behind shelter belts and walls, so as to create a garden that pretends the sea is not there. These options are often denied to the small gardener anyway.

Selecting plants

The range of plants that can be used in coastal areas becomes more extensive the further away from the sea you go. The zone just above the shoreline where there is frequent salt spray and extremely poor soil – often just sand or shingle – is the most difficult, suitable only for dedicated coastal species, such as the sea kale (*Crambe maritima*) or the colourful species of horned poppy (*Glaucium*). These are often beautiful plants in their own right, but a lot of their visual appeal derives from their environment – for instance, in the way the blue-grey of sea kale leaves tones with the austere grey of shingle and sand, or, conversely, the way the bright orange horned poppies make intense points of colour against their background.

Rocks or cliffs close to the sea are almost as difficult an environment to garden in but can be made to look exuberantly colourful with species such as the various pink-flowered thrifts (*Armeria* spp.) or the mauve daisy heads of *Erigeron glaucus*. Rocky areas that are not directly facing the sea offer more opportunity – indeed they will support a great many of the plants offered by nurseries as rockery or alpine plants.

Areas of level soil in maritime areas are often little more than sand, which means that when exposed to the sun and the wind, they are effectively semi-desert environments. The plants recommended for steppe or Mediterranean habitats (page 113) will often do well here; indeed their palette of soft foliage colours – the greys, silvers and blues – are a perfect complement to the wider environment. Many coastal habitats are dominated by either tough evergreen grasses or low shrubs, in which case a good way to continue the local theme is to choose blue-grey grasses such as *Elymus magellanicus,* or shrubs such as lavenders.

As a general rule nearly all plants that come from dry and exposed habitats, and have characteristics that indicate good resistance to desiccation and wind (see page 106) are suitable for coastal planting.

ABOVE A variety of coastal plants flourish in the lee of a shingle bank. They include *Lavatera maritima* (on the right) and the tiny daisy *Erigeron karvinskianus*.

OPPOSITE Orange-yellow California poppies (*Eschscholzia californica*) are scattered alongside other poppy species in shingle. While the poppies are annuals, surviving through scattering their seed far and wide, the sea kale (*Crambe maritima*), with large wavy-edged leaves, is a perennial, and its deep-delving roots and succulent leaves are part of its strategy for surviving desiccation and drought.

Gardening and garden design are both all too often constrained by dogma and formulaic approaches. Looking at how plants grow in the wild should open our eyes to new ways of doing things and encourage us to learn some design techniques from nature. So far we have been looking at different habitats in the garden. Now let us look at how traditional garden styles can be given a contemporary and naturalistic twist by applying nature's design lessons. Some of the most inventive and beautiful gardening in recent years has resulted from natural inspiration.

Combined with mid-season perennials such as salvia, eryngiums, *Geranium* 'Anne Folkard', a red hemerocallis cultivar and an achillea, the grass *Stipa calamagrostis* evokes the feeling of wild meadow habitats.

OPEN BORDERS

ABOVE The large pink 'daisies' of *Echinacea purpurea* and the small mauve heads of *Verbena bonariensis* are good, showy theme plants for a long late summer and early autumn season. They are joined here by thistle-like *Eryngium variifolium* and fennel (*Foeniculum vulgare*).

BELOW A steep bank makes an unconventional but spectacular setting for perennials.

We have seen how we can use ornamental plants to make areas in the garden that are almost equivalent to their wild counterparts. These are effectively miniature slices of wild habitat in the garden. But there is another way of 'natural' gardening which approaches planting style not from the direction of nature but from that of the garden – looking at how to take a conventional small garden and make it more naturalistic. Less 'natural', perhaps more conventionally ordered, even more aesthetically controlled than the plantings we have considered so far, this style involves 'mixing and matching' of plants from different habitats, with species being chosen on primarily aesthetic grounds.

This task is essentially what some contemporary garden designers have done. The much acclaimed work of Wolfgang Oehme and James van Sweden in the US, and Piet Oudolf in Europe, offers a very stylized vision of nature. The US partnership uses vast drifts of grasses and perennials to conjure up memories of the prairie, the soft textures of the grasses softening the hard outlines of buildings and paths; while Oudolf has used a wide range of plants, many never considered ornamental before, in settings that combine the traditional border format with innovative formal features. In this chapter we look at such naturalistic approaches to some traditional garden features – and at a new form, the gravel garden.

THE LIMITATIONS OF TRADITIONAL BORDERS

In most gardens, the border is the main space where the vast majority of ornamental plants are grown. The pragmatic end result of several centuries of evolution, it is a place in which to combine shrubs, herbaceous perennials and bulbs, and sometimes annuals, fruit and vegetables. In many ways the mixed border is an ideal wildlife habitat, as it offers so much diversity: shrubs for birds to roost and nest in, a dense mass of woody and herbaceous plants for wildlife to browse, well protected from predators, and a wide range of food sources. Nevertheless there is room for development. Many people have gardens that they

OPPOSITE Yellow and blue is a powerful combination for early to mid-summer. This planting, on a dry alkaline soil, features yellow *Achillea filipendulina*, blue *Veronica longifolia*, violet *Salvia nemorosa* and magenta *Lychnis coronaria*.

Coreopsis verticillata (centre) and *Rudbeckia fulgida* combine with grasses, including *Stipa gigantea* (on the right), for a romantic end-of-the-summer look.

wish were more relaxed, less suburban in feel, and they want to feel closer to nature; but they do not want a 'wild garden'. They want the garden to evoke the natural progression of the seasons but they also want colour and interest for as much of the year as possible. Are these desires contradictory?

To answer this question we need to develop a critique of the role of the border and its characteristic plants in the average garden. We can then rethink how to design the border in the small garden to be more evocative of nature, but remain a garden.

• Borders are often a strip, which in smaller gardens means they usually back on to a boundary fence, wall or hedge. Plants are to be looked at, but there is no opportunity to get in amongst them and admire them closer to. It is exceptionally difficult to plant up narrow strip borders to show plants at their best.

• Lawn often plays a major role even in smaller gardens, occupying the majority of the garden and pushing borders into their rather peripheral role.

• Many border plants are clichés of suburbia or look inherently alien, such as cypresses, which offer little to wildlife and do not change at all with the seasons. They are little more than 'green concrete'.

• Many other border plants look 'artificial': having variegated and tinted foliage, and double flowers, they are not plants that one would ever see in the wild.

• Often borders include so many different kinds of plant that the effect is messy, lacking consistency or a strong theme. An array of different flower colours, foliage shapes and textures, and plant forms and habits jostle for attention.

CHALLENGING THE LAWN

The lawn imposes a kind of tyranny over gardening. It is the dominant element in the vast majority of gardens and it is labour-intensive. Yet it is essentially featureless, a monoculture, somewhere that, even if not doused in the quantities of chemicals that many regularly apply, offers little biodiversity. Areas of grass in small gardens often suffer concentrated foot traffic and thus rarely look their best.

I think we should question the lawn's central role, in small and urban gardens in particular, and ask whether we should go to the trouble of maintaining such a biologically sterile and resource-hungry feature.

Lawns can play an important aesthetic role, as a foreground to borders, shrub plantings or a view; but in smaller gardens this is less likely to be the case than in larger gardens. Or a lawn may have a particular function – as a place for children to play on, for sunbathing, or for parties. If a lawn is not needed for any of these purposes its justification in the smaller garden is highly questionable; a lawn is a waste of space, especially if your main joy is growing a wide variety of plants.

Getting rid of the lawn is the first step towards thinking creatively about space in the garden. If you have a lawn, and decide that you can remove it, imagine the borders flowing forwards and inwards to fill up the space. The border will cease to be a strip you look *at* and instead become a more spread-out planting that you can look *over*, depending upon its height, or *through*, if there is enough space to walk through. The creative possibilities for this kind of 'open border' are very exciting, and make the conventional border seem one-dimensional in comparison.

The advantages of the open border for the small garden are many. It frees the gardener from having to think within the stereotypical pattern of 'lawn and planting around the edge' – indeed, for the smallest gardens, the border can become the garden. The open border creates a lot more space to grow a range of plants and to repeat key plants – the factor that can do more than anything else to create the sense of rhythm and unity that many conventional borders lack.

Open borders in small gardens are most suitable for small and medium-sized perennials and the kind of dwarf shrubs that make up many Mediterranean or moorland habitats. Using perennials and smaller ornamental grasses, it is possible to regard an open border, which may be as small as 4 square metres/13 square feet, as a kind of stylized meadow. Although of course plants need to be seen and appreciated as individuals, in this situation they must be small enough to create an overall effect.

REPETITION AS A DESIGN TOOL

Repetition is key to reaching this meadowy effect. Grasses, since they dominate most natural open spaces, are the best plants to use, especially since they tend to look good over a very long time. Plantings of small (20–30 cm/8–12 inches high)

Silver foliage, such as that of this *Artemisia* 'Powis Castle', works well with strong colours. This border also contains a pink *Verbascum* hybrid and the dramatic ornamental onion *Allium cristophii*.

Modern cultivars of achillea , such as 'Terracotta', shown here, work very well visually in wild-style plantings, but need light well-drained soils and reliably cold winters if they are to succeed as long-term garden plants.

perennials can be transformed by using two or three *Stipa tenuissima* every 1 square metre / 3½ square feet. Even if all the other plants are different, the feathery stipa will give the whole area a meadow-like unity for around three-quarters of the year. Larger grasses, or those with a more visually definite character, such as upward-thrusting *Molinia* cultivars, can be used with much less frequency, one every 3–4 square metres / 10–13 square feet for example, and while the effect is less meadow-like, the simple presence of a few grasses immediately evokes a hint of wild open spaces. Plants like this can be thought of as 'theme plants' that define the character of a space.

PLANT SELECTION

It is fairly obvious that many variegated or other coloured-leaf varieties are 'out'; likewise double-flowered or intensively bred-looking hybrids. But there is more that can be done to make borders look less artificial or contrived. Borders or border-type plantings can be made to look a lot more 'natural', or at least less unnatural, if a bit more discipline is exerted in plant selection, especially if the basis of selection relates to ecology.

We have seen in earlier chapters how plants that live in different environments tend to have different habits of growth: wetland plants are likely to be leafy and lush, dwellers in exposed sites small and wiry. Because of this, although mixing plants from dramatically different habitats may work in the garden, in the sense that they all flourish, it may not work visually — there may be 'too much going on' and the inconsistency in plants' growth habits may be jarring.

'Less is more' is a great design slogan. The most effective designs often consist of only a few simple motifs. In the natural-style garden this does not have to mean a restricted plant palette, but means restricting the colours or shapes used. Grey and silver foliage, for example, nearly always looks good together — not surprisingly, as the plants tend to be from similar habitats.

Wildflower meadows gain much of their visual appeal from the repetition of just a few plant species; as a consequence, the same colours and shapes are seen scattered over a wide area. Restricting colours and flower shapes as well as repeating species makes for a planting that evokes this simple meadowy feeling. Working with just a few shapes can be even more effective than restricting colour, and enables you to fit in several varieties of the same plant. For example, in a small

border you might include a number of achillea cultivars, whose disc-shaped flower heads will build up a strong visual resonance, allowing you to include several different colours.

This dry-soil planting is dominated by an eremurus, flowering above blue *Salvia nemorosa* and silver *Eryngium giganteum*. The planting shows how it is possible to create striking effects using only a very few species.

BALANCE AND FORM

Colour is the main focus for many gardeners. But in a small space form is arguably more important. Just as different colours can clash, so can different shapes, and just as colours can be harmonious, so forms can too. And in a small garden, where everything is close to hand and easily noticed, harmony is very important. Inappropriate or clashing elements will stand out.

There will be no harmony between different plant forms without balance between shapes. A dominance of low hummocky shapes, for instance, can be dull if there is no vertical interest; too many upright thrusting shapes can be restless and unsettling. Large leaves or unusual plant shapes can create interest and be a focus of attention, but if there are too many the effect can be fussy or confusing.

Shrubs tend to be amorphous in shape, and in the small garden the role of medium or large shrubs is more to do with acting as background, or in breaking up space, than being part of a composition. Smaller shrubs can often develop into pleasing rounded shapes, which, because they are permanent (not dying back in the winter), means that they maintain a sense of continuity. Low, neatly rounded hummocky shrubs like some lavenders, or santolina, can contribute an almost reassuring sense of solidity to a border.

Traditionally, gardeners have often responded to the amorphousness of shrubs by clipping them into geometric or other 'unnatural' shapes. Many who wish to garden 'naturally' may regard this practice as anathema. Others, however, may welcome the creative tension that results when a few clipped shapes, such as box, are contrasted with ebullient and wild growth. Clearly defined shapes give a garden a structure, framework and, importantly, a sense of continuity through the seasons.

Perennials have an integral form, which you can make great use of in the garden. Generally, earlier-flowering species such as cranesbill geraniums tend to be low and clump-forming, and later-flowering ones are more upright, with a much more distinctive habit. Many of these plants have great sculptural form. Think of the mid-summer-flowering monardas with their tight whorls of flower, or echinops with tight, drumstick-like flower heads, or the flat discs of achilleas. Ornamental grasses are invaluable for their wide variety of flower or seed-head shapes, some open and wispy, others dense, some upright, others loose and floppy.

A visually successful border will combine enough different shapes to create interest, but not too many to make too rich a mixture. A balance between lower clump-forming perennials and upright species is the first thing to get right. Many of the upright ones have unattractive bare stems later in the season, and will need surrounding by shorter species to hide these, as well as to provide a good visual balance. The lower-growing species are also useful for their ability to cover the surface of the soil and to deny weeds a place to grow.

Different habitats tend to be dominated by different plant forms, which contribute to the definition of their essential visual character. In trying to evoke something of these habitats in a small garden, and in using plants appropriate for the site, the 'natural' gardener can find that the predominance of one shape leads to monotony or a lack of harmony. Simply adding a few other plants with a dramatically different shape can make all the difference. Grasses are particularly

useful for this. The chart overleaf highlights some of the possible problems in particular situations and provides ideas for solutions.

POSITIONING PLANTS IN BORDERS

In traditional borders – those with a backdrop – gardeners tend to grow plants on a gradient, with the tallest at the back and the shortest at the front. This basically makes sense, as it ensures that everything is clearly visible. However, for a natural look a gradient can look too 'tidy'. Introducing a few tall but narrow plants near the front can help loosen it up; foxgloves (*Digitalis* spp.) and mulleins (*Verbascum* spp.) are two of the most useful plants for this, as they make a dramatic visual statement but take up hardly any room, and when they subsequently self-sow they will further contribute to a natural effect.

Open borders do not have a backdrop, so cannot be angled in the same way as conventional borders. One of the key visual effects we want, in order to get something of the feeling of a natural environment, is to be able see over the planting, as one can a wildflower meadow or moorland, and see various plants dotted around. So it is essential to choose species whose height will be considerably well below eye level. In small plantings, we need to be very careful about sideways spread and bulk as well. The effect will be achieved much better by having lots of smaller plants than with fewer big ones.

PLANTING FOR A LONG SEASON

Most of us want our gardens to look as good as possible for as long as possible, but recognize that in a world dominated by seasons this is unrealistic. Gardeners who are in tune with the natural world welcome the seasons and enjoy the feeling that there is a period of rest, to be followed by rebirth and then fruitful abundance and decay. After all, without a winter, there would be no spring. Rarely, however, are we happy with a garden that offers us nothing in the winter. And we will not all be satisfied with plantings that have a short season of interest. In many ways, the smaller the garden, the more hard-working it has to be. The limited space makes it essential that plants have a good long season.

Grasses planted at intervals help to create a strongly naturalistic impression. Here, in the background on the right is *Calamagrostis* x *acutiflora* 'Karl Foerster', a very upright species with a long season of interest. The yellow daisy in the foreground is *Anthemis tinctoria*.

DESIGN IDEAS FOR PROBLEMS WITH PLANT FORMS				
Garden Situation	Habitat Plants Chosen From	Predominant Plant Forms	Possible Design Problems	Adding Interest
Shade	Woodland	Low-growing	Monotonous carpet	A few taller ferns or plants with distinctive foliage
Sun	Meadow, prairie	Upright-growing	All uprights	Leave space for shorter hummocky plants or plants with distinctive leaves
Moist soil	Marshes, wet meadow	Lush, leafy	Jumble of different shapes	Ensure that there are some theme plants for a unified effect
Hot dry soil	Mediterranean scrub	Low hummocky	Lack of variation in shapes	Add grasses or others with strong form
Acid soil	Moorland, pine barrens	Low hummocky	Lack of variation in shapes	Add grasses or others with strong form

We have seen, whilst looking at various habitats that can offer inspiration for the smaller garden, that some offer more seasonal interest than others. Mediterranean habitats, with their predominance of grey-foliaged evergreens, can look good all year long, their spring and early-summer flowering being almost the icing on the cake, but wetland habitats are often dull in winter and spring, as virtually all the plants are deciduous. However, if in our planting we do not attempt to be too true to a particular natural habitat, we can, to some extent, bring plants together from different environments to ensure that we have something of interest all year long. The best way to think about seasonal interest is to consider some plant groups.

Evergreens

These are perhaps too often used: the dark green, never-changing foliage of some can be oppressively dreary and, besides, a large number, including many conifers, offer little to wildlife. Small-growing evergreens, including many

Mediterranean and acid-soil shrubs, are more useful, as their size enables them to be integrated effectively with perennials and grasses.

Multipurpose shrubs

There is little room for medium-sized or large shrubs in smaller gardens, which means the vast majority of those available commercially. The fact that many have one brief season of glory makes them even less suitable. Most useful are those species that flower in spring and are again a source of interest in autumn, with fruit or berries. Fortunately many of the species that are most useful to wildlife fall into this category. Locally native species of *Viburnum, Sorbus* or *Malus*, for instance, will link your garden to nearby landscape, look attractive and feed wild birds.

Bulbs

Since there is little room in a small garden for spring-flowering shrubs, the role of bulbs is particularly important. There are few places where robust bulbs, such as *Narcissus, Crocus* or *Galanthus* species, will not thrive, deep or evergreen shade and waterlogged soil being the main two.

Evergreen and semi-evergreen perennials

The seasonally dynamic character of herbaceous perennials is one of their joys, and it is at the core of the contemporary open-border style. The downside is that they can leave the ground very bare in late winter and spring. However, a few perennials – some epimediums and hellebores – have long-lasting leaves that make them effectively evergreen, while the small grassy liriope and ophiopogon are true evergreens. All have good-looking foliage, and can give the winter border a real lift.

Perennials with seed heads

Many perennials have seed heads that last into at least the first part of winter, which makes them invaluable for the small garden. For example, varieties of *Monarda,* and *Phlomis russeliana* have tight whorled seed heads spaced out on upright stems and can look quite dramatic as points of contrast to surrounding collapsing autumnal vegetation. The tight spires of mulleins (*Verbascum* spp.), the prickly heads of *Eryngium* species and the disc-like heads of umbellifers are all invaluable too. In addition, seed-eating birds will relish their contents.

Evergreen sedges, such as the *Carex comans* in the centre here, are very useful theme plants for open borders, happy in a wide range of conditions.

131

Grasses are among the best garden plants for winter special effects, because, unlike many flowering perennials, they withstand wet weather well. They are magically transformed by hoar frost.

Grasses

Of all herbaceous plants, grasses are the best for continuity and a long season. While some may collapse in early winter, many others will carry on looking good until the very end of the winter. Be careful to choose smaller varieties, though, especially of the popular *Miscanthus sinensis*, or the garden will be overwhelmed.

ANNUAL MEADOWS

In many regions with a seasonally arid climate, annuals play an important and colourful role. Seasonal rains cause buried seed to germinate, and this leads, within just a couple of months, to a brilliant display of colour. These annuals tend to die quickly, but not before setting copious amounts of seed to start off the next generation. Since their lives are so short and geared towards reproduction, annuals from these regions channel a larger proportion of their energies into flowers than longer-lived species of more consistently moist climates.

Not surprisingly, certain of these colourful plants have been popular with gardeners for centuries. On the whole, however, their uses in gardens have been relatively formal — often very formal, as in the case of the nineteenth-century bedding-plant tradition, which is still alive in many public parks. Even in the informal cottage-garden tradition, annuals are often still grown in unnatural-looking blocks rather than intensely intermingled as they grow in nature. Recently, though, gardeners have begun experimenting with mixing annuals together to create a naturalistic meadow effect. The results, which typically use between three and ten species, can be spectacular, evoking the exuberance and insouciance of wildflowers growing wild.

While there are a number of commercial annual seed mixes available, some of which are based around colour schemes, this is still a very young field, wide open for research and experimentation, and gardeners may prefer to try their own mixes. There are also a lot of newly introduced annuals on the market, both wild species and selections that are still close enough to the wild forms to look reasonably natural. Perhaps more than in any other area, there is scope here for the adventurous gardener to create something really new. The plant directory lists the more commonly available species (see pages 172–3), but there are many more.

Because of their speed of growth and the range and intensity of their colours, annuals are ideal for filling in spaces with temporary plantings, and for creating plantings that can be changed on an annual basis – with a different colour scheme every year perhaps. Since they tend to be small, and have a loose habit that enables them to intermingle more than perennials, they are easier to use in small spaces, and develop more readily the complex mix of species (and therefore colours) of wild plant communities. Nevertheless, they work best in broad bands rather than narrow strips. In practical terms this means areas of at least 1 square metre/3½ square feet.

Designing annual plantings involves selecting species that are compatible in height and spread, and which will look good together when flowering. Some annuals flower for a relatively short time, so it is important that for the full effect of a colour scheme to be appreciated the species chosen should flower together. Others flower for months, and in mild climates can carry on flowering until early winter. Including some of these in the garden will do much to cheer it up on dull autumn days. The inclusion of a few species for structure or texture adds another dimension: well-known annual grasses such as *Briza maxima* or *Lagurus ovatus*, for example, or a few dramatically taller plants like varieties of *Amaranthus*, or the red-leaved orache (*Atriplex hortensis* var. *rubra*).

Eryngium giganteum is a biennial which readily self-sows on most soils, even thriving on dry ones. Its bold silver-white flower heads are very distinctive scattered among other plants, while the stiff stems and seed heads last some way into winter.

Creating annual meadows

Large-scale annual meadows are big enough to visually absorb mistakes, as when perhaps one plant species forms large patches at the expense of others, or where flowering ends prematurely. Those with small gardens cannot afford many such mistakes and need to ensure that their annual meadows achieve as good a mix as possible, with a long period of flowering.

Annuals have a tendency to 'burn out' – to flower spectacularly, seed and then die. This is what they are programmed to do in the often dry habitats they come from. However, if given good conditions – moisture and a fertile soil – many will carry on flowering for many months. So it is worthwhile ensuring that soil to be used for an annual meadow is reasonably fertile and will hold moisture during dry periods. The addition of a general fertilizer and plentiful organic matter should ensure that conditions remain favourable for flowering. It is also important to sow thinly, and then to make sure that plants are well spaced out, as plants growing cheek by jowl will compete for nutrients. As a general rule, seedlings should be thinned out to no less than 20 cm/8 inches apart. Sowing is generally done in spring, just as the weather begins to warm up.

Actaea simplex is a tall and dramatic plant, flowering in late summer and autumn with heads packed with tiny flowers. It needs cool conditions to stay healthy. Light shade with a reasonably moist but well-drained soil is ideal.

Sometimes annual meadows resow themselves, although the results are rarely as good second time around. To encourage this, shake dead plants thoroughly as you remove them to scatter seed, and rake the ground over. Often in areas with mild autumn and winter climates, some species germinate in the autumn. This has several advantages: the plants will start to flower earlier in the next year, and sometimes for longer too, as in the case of the popular *Nigella damascena*.

As an alternative to sowing, plants may be raised in plug trays (see page 86) and planted out at random at 20 cm/8 inch intervals. This technique will give much better results if your soil is heavy, as clay soils reduce seed germination rates. It also makes possible the use of half-hardy annuals, which have to be sown indoors, and only planted out when the danger of frost is passed. However, it should be pointed out that plug trays can take up a lot of space, and it is difficult to give such seedlings enough light unless you have a greenhouse or conservatory.

GRAVEL GARDENS

Part and parcel of contemporary garden design are gravel gardens. Essentially the idea is to cover the ground with gravel, often over a weed-suppressing fabric (technically a 'geotextile membrane'), and grow plants either in, or surrounded by, the gravel. The gravel inhibits the growth of many invasive weedy species, although interestingly the seeds of many ornamental plants germinate well in it — an advantage if you are seeking a wild-looking effect. The material is also a highly effective backdrop for many plants, its grey or sandy-brown complementing flower and foliage colours.

Clump-forming evergreens such as cistus or common sage (*Salvia officinalis*) look particularly effective surrounded by gravel. The association of stone and plant evokes hot dry climates, and many Mediterranean-climate plants with silver-grey foliage and compact shrubby habit look good, as too do many others we associate with semi-arid climates. Spiny or spiky plants, such as eryngiums, and many of the more compact grasses, complement the hummocky forms of dwarf shrubs. The thistly-looking biennial *Eryngium giganteum* is a classic gravel garden plant, its hard silver flower heads looking every inch a dry-habitat plant. Another is the long-flowering *Verbena bonariensis*, whose seeds germinate particularly well in gravel. Gravel gardens are not suitable for taller perennials, whose long bare stems cannot be effectively hidden, or those with a high turnover of leaves and stems — too much

decaying leaf matter will soon give the gravel a dirty look, and encourage weed growth. Bulbs do well though, especially those like species tulips that need high summer temperatures to ripen the bulbs.

Gravel gardens are a very modern solution to some of the age-old problems of the small garden. As we have seen, the value of a lawn is questionable (see page 124) and gravel is a good alternative. Another glory of the gravel garden is that there is no need for hard and fast edges or boundaries between walking surfaces and planting areas; instead there can be a subtle zone of transition where plants creep forward and areas of gravel reach back between plants – a bit like many paths across areas of wild dry vegetation, in fact. Gravel is also an excellent mulch for reducing water loss, keeping the soil underneath cooler than other mulching materials such as wood chips.

Repeated silver clumps of *Artemisia* 'Powis Castle' and the golden marjoram *Origanum vulgare* 'Aureum' are the key to the strong sense of rhythm in this planting. In the foreground *Allium cristophii* towers over the lower plants.

No soil does not necessarily mean no garden. As many urban dwellers have discovered, it is possible to grow a wide range of plants in containers in even the smallest back yard – light is the only absolute essential. Covering hard surfaces with plant growth can keep the city at bay, a fact now officially recognized in the many communities which actively encourage urban greening techniques such as training climbers up walls and – most surprisingly of all – covering flat roofs with 'roofgreening' plants.

This wall has been built with soil-filled holes for a selection of plants of upland and rocky habitats, including *Dianthus deltoides*, harebell (*Campanula rotundifolia*) and several succulent species of sedum.

NATURAL GARDENING WITHOUT A GARDEN

The surfaces of roofs reflect a lot of heat, so plants for such situations need to be carefully chosen. The dry-habitat *Verbena bonariensis* here is a good choice: it will flower for months and be a first-rate source of nectar for insects.

CONTAINERS AND THE SOIL-LESS GARDEN

Many people, particularly those who live in urban areas, do not have access to any soil at all. They may have only a balcony or small yard, or a garden that a previous owner has concreted or paved over. Removing such a hard surface can be very hard work, or expensive, and of course you never know what may lie underneath — there might be only poor-quality subsoil or rubble. In such cases would-be gardeners can, however, grow plants in containers or raised beds.

The issues involved in natural-style gardening in containers are pretty much the same as those for any container plant growing. Differences are more to do with the kind of plants chosen, and how they are put together. Containers are rarely large enough to fit in much of a comprehensive ecosystem — although ponds and bog gardens might be an exception. An evocation of nature is usually the most you can hope for; and you can achieve this quite simply by using plants associated with natural habitats, locally native plants, grasses and flowers that will attract butterflies.

You need to choose plants that look as good as possible for as long as possible, but at the same time avoid the artificial appearance of conventional container plants such as pelargoniums and petunias. Unfortunately, many wildflower species are unsuitable for planting in any but the largest containers and raised beds, as they often look untidy in a container, do not have the right proportions and do not flower for long enough. The wildflowers that are likely to succeed best are the smaller-growing ones characteristic of thin rocky soils: limestone meadow flowers like harebell (*Campanula rotundifolia*), for example, or steppe flowers like the various colourful and long-flowering varieties of *Salvia nemorosa*.

Many of the compact plants sold as 'alpines' are also worth considering for containers. Among larger perennials, the longer-flowering cranesbill geraniums, such as varieties of *G. endressii* and *G. × oxonianum* and modern cultivars such as 'Rozanne' are useful. Dwarf varieties of larger perennials may be suitable too.

Many of the smaller ornamental grasses make an excellent choice. They often grow well and look good in containers, they have a long season of interest and they are hauntingly evocative of wild places. *Stipa tenuissima* is an example of the kind of grass most suitable: small, with a long season of interest and the wispy look that, combined with a few elegant wildflowers, creates an instant impression of a meadow.

Most conventional summer-flowering plants for small and medium-sized containers are annuals or frost-tender perennials. Traditional breeding has focused on producing unnaturally compact-looking plants, but the range of species available has increased over the last few years, and many newly available species maintain the loose habit of the wild. These plants tend to intermingle to create a romantically 'natural' appearance. Most of the annuals listed in the plant directory on pages 172–3 would be suitable for creating this kind of effect in containers.

The golden design rule for containers is to choose a limited number of varieties and then repeat them – too many and the effect can be fussy and chaotic. A couple of long-flowering varieties with either contrasting or complementary colours make a good basis, with the addition of either a grass or a variety chosen primarily for foliage.

Raised beds can function almost as borders, but with the advantage that plants can be chosen to spill over the edge – an effect which can be turned to great

Hare's tail grass (*Lagurus ovatus*) combines with daisy-like *Xerochrysum bracteatum* (syn. *Helichrysum bracteatum*) to bring a natural air to this container planting.

ABOVE The grass *Stipa tenuissima* on the newly planted roof of a tool shed. Notice the special lightweight material in which the plants are growing. Such materials are becoming readily available as the popularity of roofgreening increases.

OPPOSITE *Sedum acre* is one of many sedum species that are extremely drought-resistant, which makes them ideal species for roofgreening.

advantage with multilevel beds. The beds will require as much attention to feeding and watering as any other containers. They do not need bottoms, and can of course be built against walls, in which case they don't need a back either, only sides and a front.

While good drainage is essential for most plants, which means that there must be holes in the bottom of the container, or at the base of the sides in a raised bed, bog plants can flourish without any drainage. Containerized bog gardens can be very dramatic, with the large leaves of species such as *Petasites japonicus* – a plant normally only seen in large landscape gardens – making great impact. You can also make a miniature pond, and plant dwarf water lilies (some need only 25 cm/10 inches or so of water).

PLANTING VERTICALLY

We have already seen that thinking vertically (see page 37) allows us to create both more space in the garden and more biodiversity. It may sometimes be possible and desirable to use climbers where there is little opportunity to grow anything else. There may be more area available vertically than there is on the flat, and what verticals (such as walls and fences) there are can often create an oppressively enclosed atmosphere. Clothing vertical spaces enables you not just to hide undesirable hard surfaces but also to turn them into lush 'green walls', surrounding you with nature. Where there is only a minimum of soil and little space, a tree or shrub may be inappropriate, but a climber can create greenery to a considerable height, while taking up minimal horizontal space.

Climbers only really grow large when they have the resources of real soil to draw on, so if your gardening is to be restricted to containers, it would be unrealistic to expect to have climbers more than 3 metres/10 feet high, and even at that they may be very dependent upon you for water. However, their roots need only a small point of entry to be able to penetrate down into the ground, and it may be possible to break open enough of a hard surface to enable them to root through and become self-sufficient. If you have a large area of wall to cover, the results will be well worth the effort.

PLANTING FLAT ROOFS

Grass roofs are a traditional feature of country buildings in Scandinavia. Recently the concept of green roofs – covered in grass or other vegetation – has taken off in a big way in mainstream construction, initially in German-speaking countries, and now in other parts of Europe and North America too. Green roofs have been shown to have considerable environmental benefits: they help to clean the air by capturing dust and soot and by neutralizing pollutants, absorbing noise and perhaps most importantly, absorbing water, so reducing run-off into storm drains, which can contribute to flooding. In some countries they are valued so highly that it has become a legal requirement for new flat roofs to be covered in vegetation. For the domestic gardener the main advantage is perhaps aesthetic: flat roofs are often ugly, and look better covered in plants. But they also help to lengthen the life of the roofing materials by eliminating damage from ultra-violet light.

Green-roof technology is quite a specialized area, utilizing a number of high-tech materials for waterproofing, water absorption, and so forth. The construction of roofs to be 'greened' needs to allow for the considerable weight of wet substrate and you will need to seek professional advice on the ability of a roof to bear the

BAT BOXES

Bats need roosting spaces just as much as birds do, but are increasingly severely short of spaces, as the old or ruined buildings which they like are demolished or restored. Bat roosting boxes can be bought ready made or easily constructed. Plans for bat boxes are available from many nature protection organizations. Bats are very sensitive to synthetic chemicals, so the wood used should not be treated with preservatives of any kind. Bat boxes can be attached, high up, to the shady side of a house or tree.

CLIMBERS AS ROOSTING AND NESTING PLACES

Evergreen climbers are few and far between, but they are extremely valuable for wildlife, especially in urban areas, as they provide roosting and nesting places that are secure from a great many predators and from the worst of the weather. Ivy (*Hedera helix*) is an ideal refuge for insect and small bird species in areas where it is native. However, do not plant it in regions where it is not native as it can be very invasive; choose other evergreen species instead. Dead trees covered in ivy are an especially good habitat. Make these safe by removing long branches, and preserve them wherever possible.

weight. There are many specialist companies that can supply the relevant materials, and an increasing number of books and websites that cater for the DIY 'green-roof' market. Here we will simply look at the basic concept of green roofs and concentrate on the aesthetics.

Contemporary green roofs are different from traditional roof gardens, as they are not designed to be walked on, except for maintenance, and indeed are designed to need the absolute minimum of care. The roof is potentially a hot, dry place, and in winter a cold, exposed one, so plants have to be carefully chosen to suit these conditions.

The lightest roofgreening involves mosses and species of sedum, which survive on as little as a 4 cm/1½ inch layer of substrate and can survive long periods of drought. Some specialist companies offer 'vegetation mats', which consist of a biodegradable matting in which tiny plants of sedum species are already growing.

An 8 cm/3 inch layer of substrate will support a 'moss, sedum, herb' vegetation, which can include the most drought-tolerant grasses, such as *Festuca*

ABOVE A variety of sedums and grasses flourishes on a green roof with a substrate only 7 cm/3 inches deep.
RIGHT City living demands creative practical thinking directed at working out how to encourage plants to grow in different situations. Here a variety of plants are growing in containers. Once constructed and planted, containers will need either very regular watering or a carefully planned irrigation system.

Campanula poscharskyana and *Erigeron karvinskianus* both thrive in the soil-less environment of drystone walls. The campanula can send out very long roots, which exploit every available crack, while the daisy spreads by seeding.

ovina, and a range of the kind of vigorous creeping plants that are often sold as 'alpines' or rockery plants, such as the dwarf bellflower (*Campanula cochleariifolia*). A 10 cm/4 inch layer can provide a home for the kind of flora that can be found on shallow limestone soils, including such species as the greater knapweed (*Centaurea scabiosa*), while a 15 cm/6 inch layer will support a veritable wildflower meadow, with *Origanum vulgare, Iris pumila* and *Leucanthemum vulgare*. Still deeper layers of substrate will support small shrubs and conifers such the mountain pine (*Pinus mugo*), as well as a wider range of grasses. These larger plantings can put a considerable loading on roofs, however, and are suitable only for heavy concrete structures such as covered garages.

Nursery-bought plants in pots usually have too deep a set of roots for it to be practicable to plant them out on roofs. However, since many rockery plants are readily propagated, gardeners can easily raise young plants from divisions or cuttings in the kind of plug trays used by bedding-plant nurseries (which can often be rescued from their rubbish skips in the summer). Wildflower seed mixes can also be sown in these plug trays.

The basic sedum-based plant communities need virtually no maintenance. Wildflower-meadow plantings on shallow substrates may not need cutting, but will look better if dead growth is removed during winter or early spring. A shallow substrate and summer drought of course minimize problems with invasive weedy species, but they do not eliminate them, and some weeding will be necessary. The main problems are likely to be aggressive perennials such as dandelions or thistles or tree and shrub seedlings, such as buddlejas and birches. You can remove shallow-rooted seedlings carefully by hand, but perennial weeds are best dealt with by spot treating with herbicide, as this will do least damage to the substrate.

PLANTING WALLS

Old drystone walls often feature a varied range of plantlife, from tiny ferns to colourful plants such as the bright mauve bellflowers that sprout out of seemingly solid stone in late spring. Likewise garden walls and steps can support a surprising number of plants if constructed without mortar, or with the minimum of mortar needed to hold the structure together. Bellflowers (*Campanula poscharskyana* and *C. portenschlagiana*) are examples of plants that have long rooting stems that can

Sedums thrive on top of walls, where their root systems grow in the very thin layer of humus left by decaying moss.

penetrate considerable distances, even running from wall to wall across the neighbourhood. More restrained are species that seed themselves into cracks, such as the clump-forming *Corydalis lutea,* with its delicately cut foliage and yellow flowers. Walls are hostile environments in many ways, which makes it difficult for many weedy species, grasses in particular, to take hold; so the field is left open for these more specialist plants.

Retaining walls, where there is more loose material between the stones or where there is earth behind the wall, will support a wider range of plants, but they may need more upkeep as well, as unwanted plants may also take hold. In a small garden they can be a particularly rewarding place to grow small plants that appreciate sharp drainage, such as alpines, dwarf bulbs or plants from Mediterranean environments.

What makes walls especially interesting is that each side has a different microclimate. The one facing the sun will be hot and dry; the opposite side, by contrast, may be shaded, only rarely seeing the sun. You come across walls where one side is so sun-baked that only drought-tolerant succulents like sempervivum or sedum species can survive, while on the other side ferns are flourishing.

GARDENING

Natural-style gardening is different in many ways from conventional gardening. In practical as well as design considerations it seeks to work with nature wherever possible, looking for the potential of a given situation and recognizing the constraints that the environment can impose. Whereas conventional gardening is orientated towards techniques and practices, natural-style gardening is perhaps more about developing intuition – particularly about whether to intervene or just to let things develop. It recognizes that nature is dynamic and has its own agenda. Once a natural-style garden has developed, the gardener becomes a conductor rather than a master, a guiding hand rather than a controlling one.

This cheerful annual planting, dominated by the tall red flax *Linum grandiflorum* var. *rubrum* and including cornflowers (*Centaurea cyanus*), California poppies (*Eschscholzia californica*) and corn marigolds (*Xanthophthalmum segetum*) is easy to establish, as all the species can be sown directly into the ground in spring, to flower within only a few months of germination.

PRACTICALITIES OF NATURAL GARDENING

I created a bog area near the pond in my garden by underlaying a 30 cm/1 foot layer of soil with pond liner, to prevent water draining away. Here blue *Iris sibirica* towers over pink *Primula japonica*.

By working with the existing conditions rather than trying to change them, by using wild plant communities as our guide as to what will work in the garden, by tolerating imperfections and by accepting a more naturalistic look, we not only make the garden more sustainable but also reduce the amount of work we have to do.

Nevertheless, although the natural garden aims to be – and generally is – low-maintenance in comparison to conventional gardens, a certain amount of intervention is necessary. For instance, there are situations where some soil inputs such as manure and compost may be needed: in exceptionally difficult conditions, for example, or perhaps to create a garden feature that will benefit the wider environment. We have to control weeds, which are perhaps the worst enemy of the natural-style garden; and plants in the natural garden need some management.

Making the garden a fulfilling place to be for people, as well as nature-friendly, is another practical challenge: it makes sense to try to reconcile human and animal needs.

SOIL PREPARATION

If our intention is to have more or less permanent plantings of shrubs, perennials and wildflowers, we do not – as in conventional gardening, when growing vegetables and annual flowers – have to cultivate the soil every year or worry about having 'perfect' soil. We just have to ensure that we have chosen the right plants and can get them growing.

In some problematic situations it may be necessary to do some soil amelioration. Such situations include shade exacerbating soil infertility, large quantities of rubble, an absence of topsoil and compaction. While subsoil may be a positive advantage for some wildflowers, such as those of thin limestone soils, it can be discouraging when growing anything that needs richer soil.

Soil may be improved by the addition of large quantities of well-rotted organic matter: manure, agricultural waste such as spent hops, or compost – home grown or from municipal composting schemes. On a small scale it may even be worth simply buying some good-quality topsoil and spreading to a depth of at least 20 cm/8 inches over well-broken-up subsoil.

Hardpans, the result of compaction, will need physically breaking up, which is a major task, especially on a small scale, where it is impossible to use heavy machinery. You will need to put the top layer of soil to one side, and break up the hardpan with a pickaxe. Surface compaction can be dealt with by digging over, and most effectively by 'double-digging': dig a trench one spit deep (that is, to the depth of one spade), dig organic matter into the second spit, and then use the top layer from the next trench to fill the first trench, and so on.

Even situations where there is absolutely nothing but rubble need not be a problem, so long as the rubble is well drained: many former industrial areas with truly horrendous 'soil' have rich and colourful spontaneous flora. You can, though, spread out a thin layer of topsoil, or sand, over the ground in which to start seed or plants. Their developing roots will then penetrate all available gaps in the rubble.

Distinct from soil improvement is preparation for planting. Traditionally this has involved much digging over and breaking up of soil, and then the digging in of organic matter and fertilizer immediately prior to planting. In fact, plants require little breaking-up of the soil, apart from in the immediate vicinity of the planting hole, with perennials needing perhaps less than shrubs. Research has shown that adding organic matter can be counterproductive, as organic matter soaks up water, which can lead to root decay; and that not adding nutrients leads to better root growth, as it forces roots to go off in search of them.

Some plants grown in lightweight composts in nurseries find it difficult to adapt to clay soils. You can overcome this by ensuring that the soil around the new plant is well broken up, as well as gently teasing out roots from the rootball.

A good general rule is that smaller plants transplant better than larger, especially into difficult soils. Where soils are difficult to work, because they are heavy or stony, planting small specimens certainly makes the task easier.

THE ART OF NATURAL GARDEN MANAGEMENT

Managing a natural-style garden is a very intuitive business — it is difficult to set down rules. It involves a lot of trial and error, and learning over time. It is important to trust your own judgment and do what you feel is right, and not to be swayed by the opinions of others. You will make mistakes, but so long as you learn from them, little harm will be done. Constant experimentation is a big part of natural gardening.

Purplish-blue *Geranium phaeum* 'Lily Lovell' is one of several geraniums that are robust enough to thrive in rough grass, even in mild-winter regions where the grass grows very strongly.

Learning how much you can let go is important – especially with vigorously self-seeding plants, or those wildflowers that are not real weeds but could become so if allowed to go wild. In my garden I have various wild species that have introduced themselves which I basically tolerate but which I have to keep a close eye on. They have a habit of popping up in bare spaces and growing amongst 'my' plants in a way that is often very attractive, and which helps to create the feeling of densely interpenetrated planting which looks 'wild'. Persian speedwell (*Veronica persica*) runs along at ground level and does not compete with anything, so I let it grow wherever it wants to. Herb Robert (*Geranium robertianum*), with its small bright pink flowers, is also very attractive, and relatively uncompetitive, but if there are too many of its seedlings it can choke slower-growing perennials, so I weed out a proportion. Cow parsley (*Anthriscus sylvestris*) is one of the commonest local wildflowers, and one year I decided to stop weeding it out of my borders. Letting it grow helps make the garden feel more a part of the locality, and its off-white makes a good background colour for early-flowering geraniums. I noticed how light its growth is, making it a relatively uncompetitive plant, but I also noticed how much it spreads through seeding. So now I am going to cut it back after flowering, to stop it seeding, to try and keep it within desirable bounds.

Sometimes I have almost regretted introducing plants into the garden. An example is giant hogweed (*Heracleum mantegazzianum*), notorious for aggressive self-seeding and for causing skin burns in hot weather. It is a magnificent plant, when carefully sited, but I found that its seedlings were a major weed problem until I started removing most of the head after flowering, to reduce the volume of seed.

Since keeping the soil covered with plants during the summer is essential, I aim as much as possible for a carpet of plants, with different species merging together to form a complex web of growth. Increasingly I am looking for very low plants that can spread among larger perennials, to form a 'bottom layer' tightly hugging the ground. *Ajuga reptans* is a good example – this is a particularly useful plant as it flowers early, is more or less evergreen, and does not mind too much if it is densely shaded by taller species.

Being ruthless is something that many new gardeners find difficult to learn, and many non-gardening friends are often shocked by my readiness to cut plants back to ground level, or to pull them out and discard them if they have overstayed their welcome. In a small garden especially, it is vital to be able to get rid of plants that overwhelm the space or too many of their neighbours. In some cases total removal may not be necessary. Many perennials can be divided, and large chunks given away.

Finally, it is important to remember that since the natural-style garden is about partnership with nature, nature must have a hand in the design. The gardener must be open to serendipity, to letting fortuitous natural processes contribute to the garden. We may want plants to grow in certain ways, but they may insist on growing in another – and there may very well be a good scientific reason for this. If so, let them get on with it and see if you like the effect. Good visual combinations often result from chance, when natural processes allow two plants to spread so that they are next to each other.

MANAGING SHRUBS

So many of the shrubs planted in gardens grow too large for them, and it is frustrating that many of our favourite spring shrubs, plants we often do not want to do without, are so bulky and greedy of our limited space. However, there are ways of limiting their size – see page 74. Do not be afraid to cut shrubs back hard: they are designed by nature to regenerate from the base.

Otherwise, shrubs require ordinary maintenance, in which selected branches or stems are taken out, to limit the size of the plant, encourage healthy young growth and create a more interesting shape. Old, less vigorous branches should be removed, as should any older branches that are getting in the way of younger ones. As a general rule, older growth tends to have more twiggy, untidy, sideways growth. Taking it out creates more space underneath and around the plant for perennials, as well as giving the plant more character. If a shrub has an attractive branching habit or good-looking bark, do not be afraid to cut away as much as is needed to display this to best effect. Debris from shrub pruning can often be shredded (it is usually possible to hire a shredder), and used as a mulch on the soil.

MANAGING PERENNIALS

Herbaceous perennials have an undeserved reputation for being hard work. This dates back to the days of herbaceous borders full of plants like Michaelmas daisies (*Aster novi-belgii*), which need a lot of attention: staking, feeding, spraying and dividing every few years. 'Modern' perennials, though, are a different matter: they are much less labour-intensive. Most are identical, or very close, to their wild

Herb Robert (*Geranium robertianum*) is one of those wildflower species that can be allowed to self-sow to a limited extent, as its colourful flowers and attractive red-tinted foliage make it very garden-worthy. However, it can spread itself around a little too freely on some soils, so a certain amount of weeding out may be necessary.

Growing perennials in borders so that there is no space between the plants by late spring will help to reduce weed problems, as few unwanted seedlings will be able to make good growth beneath densely interlocked stems. The abundant planting in these borders includes lavenders, nepetas, sedums, macleaya, *Atriplex hortensis* var. *rubra* and *Allium sphaerocephalon*.

parents, which means that they are robust, not needing staking or feeding. The majority are also long-lived, needing very little attention for years.

Keeping unwanted weedy species at bay is the main maintenance task with perennials, especially earlier in the year, before your plants have had a chance to cover the ground, forming an interlocked mesh of vegetation that stops most seed-grown weeds from developing.

Apart from weeding, perennials require two maintenance tasks: clearing away dead stems and, after a number of years, thinning out. Dead growth is best cleared away in winter, before spring bulbs begin to show. The main problem facing small garden owners is what to do with all the debris. The ideal solution is to have a compost heap and return the resultant material to the garden, in order to recycle nutrients and build up the organic content of the soil, but there may not be space. In addition, the thick stems of some of the taller perennials take a long time to rot down. A shredder is a good answer to this problem; the larger stems can be minced into smaller pieces which can then be applied to the garden as a mulch, but the softer material will often not pass through the machine and will have to be composted or otherwise disposed of. An alternative traditional practice, if you have a vegetable garden, is to bury the debris in a deep trench, and grow beans and peas on the site.

Some perennials, many of the cranesbill geraniums being good examples, form substantial clumps with time – too big for many small gardens. With most perennials dividing is hard but straightforward work. It is best to dig up the whole plant, divide it into smaller pieces and replant vigorous new material, discarding old woody pieces of root and stem. Surplus material may be given to friends or donated to community gardens. Specialist books on perennials and propagation give tips on dividing different kinds of perennials.

WEED CONTROL

The greatest enemy of the natural-style garden is the unchecked growth of 'weeds', exceptionally competitive species that are visually unattractive and, in many cases, of limited value to wildlife. Many of the most problematic weeds are not native to the areas where they grow, but seize any opportunities that human management creates to introduce and spread themselves. If left, they overwhelm our efforts and often create a plant community that is very low in biodiversity. Larger naturalistic gardens can support a certain number of weeds without a marked deterioration, but in a small garden they can be a major problem, both aesthetically and ecologically.

Since some of the most aggressive weeds are able to propagate themselves from the tiniest piece of root left in the soil – a few pieces of ground elder (*Aegopodium podagraria*) root or Japanese knotweed (*Fallopia japonica*) left behind can mean years of constant problems – as well as from buried seed, it is of the utmost importance for a new garden or planting site to be as clean of weeds as possible. Once soil is clean, most of the worst perennial weeds will not readily re-establish themselves and weeding will be confined to the easier-to-deal-with annual weeds, which germinate from seed.

While physical means of eliminating weeds can be very effective, chemical methods are often the best. There is little to be gained from clinging to 'organic' beliefs (see page 15) – contrary to what is often believed, the environmental damage caused by the appropriate use of weedkillers is minimal, and the advantages, in improving biodiversity, can be considerable.

Thymus pulegioides is one of many thymes that are good ground-hugging plants for hot dry soils, combining well with small wildflowers and fine grasses such as species of *Festuca*.

Smothering weeds with old carpet, or thick black plastic, is the most effective means of non-chemical control on a new site, with the exception of the edges, particularly around trees or structures, where often the use of an appropriate weedkiller is realistically the only way of killing them. Most non-woody weeds are easily controlled with products containing glyphosate, a chemical with an excellent safety record, and which is rapidly broken down by soil bacteria.

If the garden has been well cleared of weeds before planting, the only problem should be seedling weeds. These can be removed with a hoe whilst still small, or hand pulled once they get a bit bigger.

If weed root remnants have been left in the soil, these will be much harder to deal with, as it is very difficult to remove all the root system of a perennial weed with a running root, such as couch grass (*Elytrigia repens*) or ground elder (*Aegopodium podagraria*). Spot treatment with a glyphosate-based weedkiller early in the season, as soon as their growth has started, is the best way of dealing with these kinds of weeds, as it will kill the whole root system. Mixing weedkiller with wallpaper paste is a good trick: it enables you to paint a thick mixture on to weed stems or leaves with great precision. Later-emerging weeds such as bindweed (*Convolvulus arvensis*) can be a real problem, but the wallpaper paste and weedkiller trick will also work if you first give the bindweed a bamboo pole to climb up so that it is well separated from wanted plants.

MULCHING

Mulching means covering the surface of the soil with a layer of loose material, mainly to reduce water loss during the summer and to prevent weeds from establishing themselves. It plays a major role in modern low-maintenance planting design.

In the case of gravel mulches, the look of the material plays a role in the overall design, and the gravel garden is a garden feature in its own right (see page 134). Borders and other garden features are generally mulched with bark and wood chips, whose colour and texture allows them to blend into the surroundings.

A wood chip mulch needs to be applied at about 3–5cm / 1½–2in thick, after all planting is complete. Disturbing the soil after mulching inevitably involves mixing soil and mulch, which defeats its purpose. Be careful not to smother dormant perennials with the mulch.

Its success in weed suppression is the main reason why many gardeners use a wood chip mulch and to use it successfully it is important to understand how and why it achieves this. Mulch does not have any effect on the growth of buried weed roots, but it does very successfully inhibit the germination of buried weed seed, which every soil has, soils on new developments usually having considerable quantities. A wood chip mulch also greatly reduces the germination of weed seeds that land on the surface of the soil after planting.

A disadvantage of a wood chip mulch is that it cannot be used on slopes, or anywhere that gets flooded. It can also make it difficult for low spreading plants (such as species of *Acaena* or *Thymus*) to root into the ground. Since it provides an unsuitable surface for seed germination, it will also inhibit the long-term survival of plants that are short-lived and dependent upon sowing themselves, such as *Verbascum* and *Digitalis*.

WATERING

The irrigation of gardens is an issue of much concern, as in many places expanding populations are putting enormous pressures on water resources.

Fundamental to reducing the demands that gardening places on water resources is the selection of plants which can cope with the average levels of summer drought that can be expected in a region in an average year. This may mean that in areas where summer drought is the norm, the high summer period is not as colourful as many would wish. Most plants of dry habitats flower early and become semi-dormant during summer. Whilst your garden may be quietly attractive, with a range of evergreen plants, you may have to limit bright flower colours to irrigated containers or one small bed.

The root systems of established plants extend to considerable depths in the soil, even into cracks in the bedrock, allowing them to access moisture from a wide area. However, on artificially thin soil, for example soil overlying underground concrete structures, or where soil has been damaged during construction work, there may be only limited opportunities for plants to develop full root systems and in such cases, irrigation may be necessary.

Newly established plantings will also need irrigation during hot and dry summer weather. Even in cool climates, if you plant in spring, some summer watering will probably be necessary.

Overhead watering is very wasteful and inefficient, so when irrigating select systems that minimize overhead watering. Buried permeable hose, or even just a hose with a series of fine holes drilled into it, is far and away the best means of irrigation, as it slowly trickles water out straight to the roots and completely avoids wastage through evaporation.

LIVING SPACES

We nearly all choose to live in our gardens to some extent; only rarely is a garden somewhere that is admired or observed only from outside, from a window or the street. Living in a garden means finding somewhere for seating and dining places, and space for children to play. In a 'natural' garden, these requirements create the potential for conflict, as wildlife needs seclusion, and that may be difficult to provide in a small garden where human interests come first. However, part of the joy of a garden is in observing wildlife, so it is worth trying to reconcile human and animal needs, for instance by closely juxtaposing seating and bird-friendly undergrowth.

Throughout the ages gardens have tended to become wilder and less controlled the further away from the house they go and in many gardens the main 'living space' is adjacent to the house. This makes sense, particularly for eating, and it allows the rest of the garden to be observed, either passively as a backdrop or more intensively, for instance by birdwatching. At best this means that the living area can be surrounded on three sides by garden. However, if the garden is big enough it is rather wonderful to create a living area that is surrounded on all sides by greenery – if you live in a town, you can then live the illusion of being in the countryside. You don't need a great deal of space; only a green screen is necessary for the side that secludes the site from the house. Green screens can be made most effectively and quickly by growing climbers up trellis. Bamboo is an alternative, as it offers height and screening but does not take up much sideways space. Where there is space, shrubs may be used.

Ponds are popular places to have next to living areas, as they create a restful atmosphere and offer so many opportunities for small-scale wildlife watching. If there is any kind of slope you could have a raised brick or stone edge on the vulnerable side of the pond and yet have marginal plants on the other.

Living spaces in gardens are often 'hard', using paving or decking rather than lawn. This makes practical sense in the small garden, as the amount of wear and

tear the surface is liable to receive in a restricted space may be too much for even the toughest grass. However, the effect is all too often most unnatural. If you want to have paving, a natural stone is clearly a better choice than a man-made material. Bear in mind, though, that any kind of paving reduces the ability of the ground to absorb run-off from heavy rain, which is an environmental issue in many urban areas. The quarrying of natural stone also often has undesirable environmental and social costs too. Brick is a good alternative to stone, and often has a warmer look to it than stone.

Unlike paving, decking allows some water to pass through it and therefore be absorbed by the ground underneath. It also creates less of a disposal problem if the next owner of the property does not want it. In short it is more sustainable than paving. However, you need to be sure that the timber is from a sustainably managed source. Some timbers such as eucalyptus and 'cedar' contain natural oils which protect against decay; others have to be treated in order to preserve them. With these, avoid conventional preservatives that rely on chromium- or arsenic-based chemicals.

What is particularly good about decking is that it can be used to create flat or perhaps occasionally stepped areas over considerable changes in level, and on slopes it can be used dramatically to project a living area into mid-air. Doing this into forest or other wooded areas can offer not only visual drama but enhanced opportunities for wildlife watching.

Planting around sitting and dining areas needs to be ornamental for a long season. Temporary summer plants, which can usually be guaranteed to flower all summer long, are a popular choice for such positions. Planting them in containers allows you to move them around to create the best effect. Most of us want to have scent in living areas too. Fragrant flowers are usually relatively short-lived, however, and unfortunately for us, 'unimproved' wild species tend to flower for a shorter period than many of their hybridized offspring. Aromatic foliage continues through the growing season, though: lavenders, cistus, sages, thymes and other Mediterranean maquis flora will release a pungent scent on hot still summer days, or at any time in response to a hand brushed through the leaves.

Very wild gardens are often managed extensively, plants being treated *en masse* rather than each individually. This garden meadow will be mown at the end of the season, and possibly in mid-summer as well.

A variety of *Helleborus* x *hybridus*. Hellebores are some of the most exciting plants for woodland-edge habitats for the earliest part of the year. They flourish on any soil that does not regularly dry out.

PLANT DIRECTORY

HEIGHT AND SPREAD

The height given is the eventual height, which perennials generally reach in the second year after planting and most shrubs after 10–20 years. Where plants are growing in meadow or prairie plantings – that is, where they are very closely packed – competition is much greater, so height may be 50 per cent less.

Spread is much more difficult to define than height. For perennials the distance given is very generally that achieved after three years' growth. In practice the distances given are perhaps more usefully seen as a guide to planting distances: imagine a circle of a diameter equal to the planting distance with the plant in the centre. Many perennials will carry on spreading indefinitely, and in this case may well, in time, need to be divided or cut back.

Measurements should not be taken as definitive. It is actually quite difficult to get good data for some of the species included here. This applies particularly to the dry-habitat section.

SEASON

ESp = early spring ESu = early summer A = autumn
MSp = mid-spring MSu = mid-summer EW = early winter
LSp = late spring LSu = late summer LW = late winter
W = winter

HARDINESS ZONES

The zone ratings allocated to each plant are based on the zones of average annual minimum temperature devised by the United States Department of Agriculture and suggest the minimum temperature the plant will tolerate in winter. However, this can only be a rough guide, as hardiness depends on many factors, including the depths of a plant's roots, the duration of cold weather and the temperatures encountered during the preceding summer.

SOIL

W = wet soils – that is, subject to regular inundation or prolonged waterlogging
M = moist soils – that is, never appreciably drying out
N = 'normal' conditions – that is, soils that do not experience waterlogging or suffer prolonged drought on a regular basis
D = soils that regularly suffer some summer drought
Ac = soils that are strongly acidic, below pH6

KEY

** There are many other species or cultivars similar in size and cultural requirements. The one chosen is simply the most widely grown.
E = evergreen
semi-E = semi-evergreen
c = coastal

°Celsius	Zones	°Fahrenheit
below −45	1	below −50
−45 to −40	2	−50 to −40
−40 to −34	3	−40 to −30
−34 to −29	4	−30 to −20
−29 to −23	5	−20 to −10
−23 to −18	6	−10 to 0
−18 to −12	7	0 to 10
−12 to −7	8	10 to 20
−7 to −1	9	20 to 30
−1 to 4	10	30 to 40
above 4	11	above 40

PLANTS FOR WOODLAND SHADE

Here N = more precisely normal soil that is well drained but never dries out, staying cool and moist to the touch through the summer
In the cooler climates of higher latitudes and altitudes many of these plants will thrive in light shade

Perennials	Height and spread	Habit	Flowers	Season	Soil	Zone	Remarks
Actaea rubra **	45cm/18in × 30cm/12in	clump-forming	white	MSp, ESu	N	4	shiny red berries
Arisaema triphyllum **	60cm/24in × 15cm/6in	tuberous	green spathe	Sp, ESu	N	4	clusters of red berries
Arum italicum 'Pictum'	30cm/12in × 30cm/12in	clump-forming	pale green spathes	Sp	N	6	patterned leaves
Asarum hartwegii **	8cm/3in × 30cm/12in	prostrate E	brownish purple	ESu	N	5	bronze, marbled leaves
Dicentra eximia	30cm/12in × 45cm/18in	clump-forming	pink, white	Su	N	4	greyish ferny foliage
Galax urceolata	30cm/12in × 100cm/40in	tufted E	white spikes	LSp, ESu	N, Ac	5	round, glossy leaves
Helleborus foetidus	80cm/32in × 45cm/18in	erect E	greenish	LW	N D	4	lobed leaves
Meconopsis cambrica	40cm/16in × 25cm/10in	erect	yellow	ESu	N	6	self-seeds
Omphalodes verna	15cm/6in × 30cm/12in	clump-forming	clear blue	Sp	N	5	spreads slowly

Perennials	Height and spread	Habit	Flowers	Season	Soil	Zone	Remarks
Podophyllum peltatum	45cm/18in × 120cm/48in	creeping	white, pale pink	MSp, ESu	N	4	glossy leaves
Polygonatum × hybridum **	60cm/24in × 30cm/12in	elegant, arching	white	Su	N	4	summer dormant
Pulmonaria saccharata	30cm/12in × 60cm/24in	clump-forming E	pink, blue	Sp	M N	4	white-spotted leaves
Saxifraga fortunei (and hybrids)	30cm/12in × 30cm/12in	clump-forming	white sprays	LSu, A	N	7	attractive range leaf tones
Tiarella wherryi **	20cm/8in × 15cm/6in	clump-forming	white, pink tinged	LSp, ESu	M N	6	maroon-tinted leaves
Trillium grandiflorum	30cm/12in × 30cm/12in	clump-forming	white	Sp	N	4	slow to increase
Uvularia grandiflora	75cm/30in × 30cm/12in	spreading	yellow	MSp, LSp	N	3	perfoliate, hairy leaves
Vinca minor	15cm/6in × indefinite	spreading E	blue	Sp	N D	4	glossy leaves
Viola canina **	15cm/6in × 30cm/12in	decumbent	blue, violet	Sp, ESu	M N	6	heart-shaped leaves
Waldsteinia ternata	10cm/4in × 60cm/24in	spreading semi-E	yellow	Sp	N D	3	lobed, toothed leaves

Grasses/Grass-like	Height and spread	Habit	Flowers	Season	Soil	Zone	Remarks
Carex plantaginea	25cm/10in × 30cm/12in	dense tufts	tight leafy clumps E		N D	7	strap-shaped leaves
Chasmanthium latifolium	100cm/40in × 60cm/24in	tufts	green, oat-like	LSu, A	N	4	yellow winter foliage
Luzula nivea	60cm/24in × 45cm/18in	spreading E	pure white	ESu, MSu	N	6	
Melica nutans	45cm/18in × 30cm/12in	creeping	brown and cream	LSp, MSu	N	6	fresh green foliage

Bulbs and tubers	Height and spread	Habit	Flowers	Season	Soil	Zone	Remarks
Anemone nemorosa **	10cm/4in × 30cm/12in	creeping	white, pink flushed	Sp	N	4	lobed, toothed leaves
Convallaria majalis	20cm/8in × 30cm/12in	spreading	white	Sp	N	4	rich fragrance
Cyclamen coum **	8cm/3in × 10cm/4in	clumps	white, pink	W, Esp	N D	6	leaves sometimes marked
Cyclamen hederifolium **	10cm/4in × 15cm/6in	clumps	white, pink	LSu, A	N D	6	leaves may be marked
Erythronium dens-canis **	15cm/6in × 10cm/4in	clumps	pink, white,	Sp	N	3	American spp. yellow
Galanthus nivalis	10cm/4in × 10cm/4in	clumps	white	Sp	N D	4	narrow, greyish leaves

Ferns	Height and spread	Habit	Flowers	Season	Soil	Zone	Remarks
Adiantum pedatum	30cm/12in × 30cm/12in	creeping			N	3	graceful fronds
Asplenium scolopendrium	30cm/12in × 60cm/24in	creeping E			N D	4	leathery, undivided fronds
Asplenium trichomanes	15cm/6in × 20cm/8in	creeping E			N D	4	
Asplenium ceterach	15cm/6in × 20cm/8in	tufted E			N D	8	rounded, lobed fronds
Athyrium filix-femina	60cm/24in × 60cm/24in	erect			N	4	delicate fresh green fronds
Dryopteris filix-mas **	100cm/40in × 100cm/40in	sturdy semi-E			N D	4	most robust fern
Matteuccia struthiopteris	100cm/40in × 100cm/40in	vase-shaped			M N	2	excellent for damp
Polypodium vulgare	30cm/12in × indefinite	erect E			N D	3	deeply divided fronds
Polystichum munitum	90cm/36in × 120cm/48in	shuttlecocks E			N D	5	big but good under trees
Polystichum setiferum	50cm/20in × 90cm/36in	shuttlecocks E			N D	5	intricately divided fronds

PLANTS FOR WOODLAND EDGE – LIGHT SHADE/SUN

In the cooler climates of higher latitudes and altitudes many of these plants will thrive in full sun

Perennials	Height and spread	Habit	Flowers	Season	Soil	Zone	Remarks
Aconitum napellus **	150cm/60in × 30cm/12in	erect	indigo-blue	MSu, LSu	M N	6	toothed and lobed leaves
Ajuga reptans	10cm/4in × 75cm/30in	creeping E	clear blue	Sp	M N	3	shiny bronzy foliage
Alchemilla mollis	40cm/16in × 75cm/30in	dense clumps	lime-green	ESu	M N D	4	elegant foliage
Anemone × hybrida vars.	100cm/40in × 100cm/36in	upright	pink, white	LSu, A	M N	5	many varieties

Perennials	Height and spread	Habit	Flowers	Season	Soil	Zone	Remarks
Actaea racemosa **	80cm/32in × 60cm/24in	clump-forming	white	Su, A	M	3	dislikes competion
Aquilegia canadensis	75cm/30in × 30cm/12in	erect	scarlet and yellow	MSp, ESu	M N	3	divided leaves
Aquilegia vulgaris	70cm/28in × 45cm/18in	erect	blue, pink	ESu	N	5	greyish, divided leaves
Aruncus dioicus 'Kneiffii'	150cm/60in × 120cm/48in	robust clumps	cream	Su	M N	3	fern-like foliage
Aster cordifolius	100cm/40in × 45cm/18in	clump-forming	pale to deep blue	LSu, A	M N	3	
Aster divaricatus	70cm/28in × 60cm/24in	clump-forming	white	LSu	N D	4	dark stems
Aster macrophyllus	60cm/24in × 60cm/24in	clump-forming	pale lilac	A	N D	3	handsome leaves
Astrantia major	80cm/32in × 45cm/18in	clump-forming	cream, reddish	Su	M N	4	lobed, toothed leaves
Buphthalmum salicifolium	60cm/24in × 45cm/18in	clump-forming	yellow daisies	ESu to A	N D	4	willow-like leaves
Calamintha grandiflora	45cm/18in × 45cm/18in	bushy	pink	Su	M N D	5	aromatic leaves
Campanula latifolia	80cm/32in × 60cm/24in	upright, loose	lilac	MSu	N D	4	*C. trachelium* similar
Campanula persicifolia	60cm/24in × 30cm/12in	rosettes E	blue, white	MSu	N D	4	especially good on sand
Chaerophyllum hirsutum 'Roseum'	60cm/24in × 40cm/16in	erect	pink umbels	LSp, Su	M N	6	very divided foliage
Chrysogonum virginianum	30cm/12in × 60cm/24in	creeping	yellow daisy	Sp, ESu	N	6	variable growth
Doronicum orientale **	50cm/20in × 90cm/36in	spreading	yellow daisy	ESu	N	5	other species similar
Eupatorium rugosum	100cm/40in × 60cm/24in	clump-forming	white	LSu, A	N	4	nettle-like leaves
Euphorbia characias	150cm/60in × 120cm/48in	erect, bushy E	yellow-green	LW, ESp	N D	7	thrives amongst tree roots
Gentiana triflora	45cm/18in × 25cm/10in	erect	purple-blue	LSu, A	N Ac	5	
Geranium clarkei	50cm/20in × 60cm/24in	spreading	purple-violet	ESu to LSu	M N D	4	deeply divided leaves
Geranium endressii	70cm/28in × 70cm/28in	clumps semi-E	pink	ESu to A	M N	4	weed-smothering foliage
Geranium macrorrhizum	40cm/16in × 60cm/24in	spreading semi-E	pink, white	ESu	N D	4	weed-smothering foliage
Geranium × oxonianum	70cm/28in × 80cm/32in	spreading	pink	ESu to A	M N	4	many different hybrids
Geranium sylvaticum	60cm/24in × 60cm/24in	clump-forming	pink, mauve	ESu	M N	4	many colour forms
Geranium wallichianum 'Buxton's Variety'	30cm/12in × 120cm/48in	spreading	blue, white centre	MSu to A	N D	4	
Helleborus × hybridus	45cm/18in × 45cm/18in	erect	cream, grey, red	LW, ESp	N	6	
Heuchera micrantha **	90cm/36in × 45cm/18in	mound-forming	white, pink flushed	ESu	N	5	grey-marbled leaves
Iris cristata	10cm/4in × 20cm/8in	erect	lavender	LSp	N	6	
Iris douglasiana	30cm12in × 50cm/20in	tufted	cream, blue, mauve	LSp, ESu	N	8	
Kirengeshoma palmata	100cm/40in × 75cm/30in	clump-forming	pale yellow	LSu, A	M Ac	5	large, lobed leaves
Lamium maculatum cvs.	20cm/8in × 100cm/40in	spreading E	purple, pink, white	Sp	N D	3	silver/gold-marked leaves
Lamium orvala	60cm/24in × 30cm/12in	clump-forming	pinkish purple	LSp, Su	N D	6	non-invasive
Libertia formosa **	90cm/36in × 60cm/24in	clump-forming	white, pale yellow	LSp, MSu	N	8	linear, leathery leaves
Lunaria rediviva	60cm/24in × 50cm/20in	bushy	palest lilac	Sp to ESu	M N	4	fragrant
Melittis melissophyllum	50cm/20in × 50cm/20in	erect	white and pink	LSp, ESu	M N	6	nettle-like leaves
Myrrhis odorata	90cm/36in × 60cm/24in	erect	white	ESu	M N	4	a tame 'cow parsley'
Phlox paniculata	180cm/72in × 80cm/32in	clump-forming	pale pink	Su	M N	4	parent of garden hybrids
Phlox stolonifera	30cm/12in × 30cm/12in	trailing	pink, blue	ESu	N Ac	3	*P. divaricata* similar
Pimpinella major 'Rosea'	120cm/48in × 60cm/24in	erect	deep and pale pink	ESu, MSu	N	5	like a pink 'cow parsley'
Primula elatior	20cm/8in × 25cm/10in	rosettes E	pale yellow	Sp	N	5	
Primula japonica **	60cm/24in × 45cm/18in	rosettes	pink, white	ESu	M N	6	good self-seeder
Salvia glutinosa	100cm/40in × 90cm/36in	robust clumps	pale yellow	Su	N D	5	
Selinum wallichianum	150cm/60in × 60cm/24in	clump-forming	white umbels	MSu to A	N	5	elegant umbellifer
Senecio nemorensis	180cm/72in × 60cm/24in	upright	yellow	MSu to LSu	N D	5	good under trees
Silene dioica	80cm/32in × 45cm/18in	clumps semi-E	bright pink	ESu	M N	5	good self-seeder
Tricyrtis formosanum **	80cm/32in × 45cm/18in	erect	white, spotted pink	EA	M N	7	leaves spotted purplish green

Biennials and short-lived perennials	Height and spread	Habit	Flowers	Season	Soil	Zone	Remarks
Anthriscus sylvestris	80cm/32in × 30cm/12in	clump-forming	white umbels	MSp, Esu	N	5	fern-like foliage
Bupleurum falcatum	90cm/36in × 60cm/24in	clump-forming	yellow-green	Su	N D	3	
Digitalis ferruginea	120cm/48in × 45cm/18in	rosettes E	golden brown	Msu	N D	4	seed heads good in winter
Digitalis grandiflora	100cm/40in × 45cm/18in	clump-forming E	pale yellow	ESu, Msu	N D	4	
Digitalis purpurea	150cm/60in × 30cm/12in	rosettes E	white to purple	Su	N D	4	thrives in full sun
Geranium pyrenaicum	30cm/12 × 50cm/18in	sprawling E	lilac	Sp to A	N D	7	

Bulbs and tubers	Height	Habit	Flowers	Season	Soil	Zone	Remarks
Hyacinthoides non-scripta	20cm/8in	clump-forming	violet blue, white	LSp	N Ac	4	broadly grassy foliage
Leucojum aestivum	60cm/24in	erect	white, green tips	LSp	M N	4	strap-shaped glossy leaves
Lilium martagon	120cm/48in	clump-forming	pink, purple	ESu	N	4	may self-seed
Narcissus cyclamineus	20cm/8in	erect	golden yellow	Esp	N	4	
Narcissus pseudonarcissus	25cm/10in	erect	yellow	LSp	N	4	many hybrids
Scilla siberica **	15cm/6in	semi-erect	blue	Sp	N	3	

Grasses and sedges	Height and spread	Habit	Flowers	Season	Soil	Zone	Remarks
Carex morrowii	30cm/12in × 40cm/16in	dense tufts E			M N	7	also variegated forms
Carex muskingumensis	60cm/24in × 30cm/12in	upright, tufted			M N	4	palm-like habit
Deschampsia cespitosa	200cm/80in × 120cm/48in	tussock-forming E	silver and purple	ESu to LSu	N	5	
Sesleria autumnalis	40cm/16in × 40cm/16in	upright, tufted E			N	5	also good on acid soils

Shrubs	Height and spread	Habit	Flowers	Season	Soil	Zone	Remarks
Amelanchier lamarckii **	10m/30ft × 12m/40ft	wide branching	white clusters	MSp	M N	4	orange/red autumn foliage, purple fruit
Aronia prunifolia **	3m/10ft × 2.5m/8ft	erect, suckering	white	LSp	M N	4	purple/red autumn foliage, dark purple berries
Betula pendula **	25m/80ft × 10m/30ft	narrow canopy	yellow catkins	ESp	M N D	1	yellow autumn foliage
Buddleja davidii	3m/10ft × 5m/16ft	upright, arching	lilac, purple	LSu, A	N D	5	attractive to butterflies
Clethra alnifolia	2.5m/8ft × 2.5m/8ft	upright, suckering	white, fragrant	LSu, A	M N Ac	3	remove old wood in winter
Cornus mas **	5m/15ft × 5m/16ft	spreading	yellow umbels	LW	N	5	bright red fruits late summer
Crataegus monogyna **	10m/30ft × 8m/25ft	rounded	white, fragrant	LSp	N	5	thorny stems, dark red fruits autumn
Euonymus americanus **	3m/10ft × 3m/10ft	spreading shape	yellow-green	A (fruits)	M N	6	pink, warty fruits, flowers insignificant
Hydrangea quercifolia	2m/6½ft × 2.5m/8ft	mound-forming	white panicles	MSu to A	M N	5	bronze-purple foliage autumn
Ilex aquifolium **	25m/80ft × 8m/25ft	erect, dense E	pink tinged	W (fruits)	N	6	spiny leaves, red berries, flowers insignificant
Ilex verticillata **	5m/16ft × 5m/16ft	suckering	white	MSp	N	3	berries red, orange or yellow
Mahonia aquifolium **	1m/40in × 1.5m/5ft	suckering E	yellow	Sp	M N	5	spiny leaves, blue-black berries
Oemleria cerasiformis	2.5m/8ft × 4m/13ft	suckering	white, fragrant	ESp	M N	6	plum-like, purple-black fruits on females
Potentilla fruticosa	1m/40in × 1.5m/5ft	compact, bushy	yellow	LSp to A	N D	5	many different varieties
Prunus mume	9m/30ft × 9m/30ft	spreading	white, pink	LW, ESp	M N	6	yellow, apricot-like fruits
Prunus tenella	1.5m/5ft × 1.5m/5ft	upright	bright pink	Sp	M N	2	grey-yellow, almond-like fruits
Prunus triloba	3m/10ft × 3m/10ft	densely branched	pink	Sp	M N	5	spherical red fruits
Ribes sanguineum	2m/6½ft × 2m/6½ft	upright	deep pinkish red	Sp	N D	5	aromatic leaves, glaucous, blue-black fruits

Shrubs	Height and spread	Habit	Flowers	Season	Soil	Zone	Remarks
Rosa canina **	5m/15ft × 1m/40in	arching	white, pale pink	Su	N	3	prickly stems, waxy, bright red fruits
Rosa carolina **	1.5m/5ft × indefinite	upright, suckering	pink	Su	N	4	prickly stems, red, bristly fruits
Sambucus nigra **	6m/20ft × 6m/20ft	upright, bushy	white	ESu	M N	5	clusters of glossy black fruits
Sorbus aucuparia **	15m/50ft × 7m/23ft	conical to rounded	white	LSp	M N	2	orange-red berries
Viburnum cassinoides **	2.5m/8ft × 2m/6½ft	upright	yellow-white	Su	M N	2	autumn foliage red, fruits blue-black
Viburnum lantana **	5m/15ft × 4m/13ft	upright	white clusters	LSp, ESu	M N	3	autumn foliage red, fruits red then black

Climbers	Height and spread	Habit	Flowers	Season	Soil	Zone	Remarks
Aconitum volubile **	3m/10ft	twining, scrambling	purple	MSu to EA	M N	2	large, lobed, hairy leaves
Clematis viticella **	3m/10ft	leaf-stalk climber	blue, purple, red	MSu to EA	M	6	attractive seed heads
Dicentra macrantha	60cm/24in × 45cm/18in	spreading	creamy yellow	LSp	M	6	may be damaged by late frosts
Hedera helix	10m/30ft	self-clinging E	yellow-green	A	M N	5	glossy, lobed, dark green leaves
Lonicera periclymenum **	7m/23ft	twining	white to yellow	MSu, LSu	M N	4	bright red berries in autumn

PLANTS FOR GRASSLAND – MEADOW

Perennials	Height and spread	Habit	Flowers	Season	Soil	Zone	Remarks
Achillea millefolium	60cm/24in × 60cm/24in	creeping E	white clusters	Su	M N D	3	feathery foliage
Anthericum liliago	50cm/20in × 30cm/12in	clump-forming	white	ESu	N D	6	grass-like foliage
Aster linosyris	60cm/24in × 30cm/12in	clump-forming	yellow	LSu	D	3	finely divided leaves
Campanula glomerata	60cm/24in × 60cm/24in	spreading	purple-blue	ESu	N D	3	prone to slugs
Campanula rotundifolia	15cm/6in × 15cm/6in	creeping	blue	Su	N D	3	dislikes competition
Centaurea nervosa	100cm/40in × 60cm/24in	robust clumps	pink-mauve	Su	N	4	many similar wild spp.
Centaurea nigra	60cm/24in × 30cm/12in	small clumps	mauve-pink	Su	N D	5	tough and adaptable
Centaurea scabiosa	70cm/28in × 30cm/12in	basal rosettes	carmine pink	Su	D	4	very showy
Centaurium erythraea	15cm/6in × 2.5cm/1in	rosettes	bright pink, tiny	Su	N D	3	dislikes competition
Cichorium intybus	80cm/32in × 60cm/24in	upright	clear blue	Su	N D	4	biennial
Daucus carota	80cm/32in × 20cm/8in	upright	off-white heads	Su	N D	3	often self-seeds
Dianthus carthusianorum	50cm/20in × 20cm/8in	tufted	deep pink, red	Su	D	3	showy
Euphorbia cyparissus	30cm/12in × indefinite	spreading	greeny-yellow	Su	D	3	finely divided leaves
Filipendula vulgaris	50cm/20in × 45cm/18in	rosettes	creamy-white	ESu	N D	4	finely divided leaves
Galium verum	40cm/16in × 30cm/12in	scrambling	yellow heads	Su	N D	3	finely divided leaves
Geranium phaeum	50cm/20in × 60cm/24in	clump-forming	maroon, pink	LSp	M N	4	good in rough grass
Geranium pratense	70cm/28in × 60cm/24in	upright	mauve-blue	Su	M N D	4	good in rough grass
Hippocrepis comosa	20cm/8in × indefinite	creeping	yellow, pea-like	ESu	D	6	
Hypericum perfoliatum	60cm/24in × 60cm/24in	erect	yellow	Su	N	3	
Iris graminea	30cm/12in × 20cm/8in	erect	pale violet	ESu	D	5	grassy foliage
Jasione laevis	30cm/12in × 20cm/8in	dense tufts	lavender	Su	N D	5	dark green leaves
Knautia arvensis	60cm/24in × 30cm/12in	rosettes	pale lavender	Su	N D	6	
Lathyrus pratensis	70cm/28in × 200cm/80in	scrambling	yellow, pea-like	ESu	N D	4	several other species
Leucanthemum vulgare	60cm/24in × 60cm/24in	spreading	white and yellow	ESu	N D	3	short-lived
Linaria vulgaris	30cm/12in × 30cm/12in	sprawling	yellow 'snapdragons'	Su	D	4	

Perennials	Height and spread	Habit	Flowers	Season	Soil	Zone	Remarks
Linum perenne	25cm/10in × 15cm/6in	bunched stems	pale clear blue	ESu	D	4	
Lotus corniculatus	15cm/6in × 30cm/12in	spreading	yellow, pea-like	ESu	N D	5	
Malva moschata	60cm/24in × 60cm/24in	shrubby	pale pink, large	Su	N D	4	divided leaves
Mentha longifolia	70cm/28in × 100cm/40in	creeping	pale pink	Su	W M N	6	grey leaves
Onobrychis viciifolia	60cm/24in × 40cm/16in	lax stems	dusky pink	ESu	N D	6	striking colour
Ononis repens	20cm/8in × 60cm/24in	compact	strong pink	Su	N D	6	best on drier soils
Origanum vulgare	30cm/12in × 30cm/12in	shrubby	dull pink	Su	D	4	aromatic leaves
Persicaria bistorta	80cm/32in × 90cm/36in	spreading	pink	ESu	M N	4	dock-like leaves
Phyteuma orbiculare	30cm/12in × 30cm/12in	erect	deep blue, spiky	ESu	M N D	6	
Pilosella aurantiaca	25cm/10in × 90cm/36in	dense mats	dull orange	ESu	M N	4	can be invasive
Polemonium caeruleum	60cm/24in × 30cm/12in	clump-forming	clear blue	ESu	M N	4	can seed widely
Primula veris	15cm/6in × 15cm/6in	rosettes E	yellow	Sp	N D	5	good spring plant
Prunella vulgaris	20cm/8in × 30cm/12in	low-growing	violet-purple	Su	M N D	6	thrives in lawns
Ranunculus acris	70cm/28in × 22cm/9in	erect clumps	bright yellow	LSp, Su	M N D	4	easy and adaptable
Reseda lutea	60cm/24in × 30cm/12in	erect	creamy-yellow	Su	N D	6	short-lived, fragrant
Salvia pratensis	60cm/24in × 30cm/12in	clump-forming	deep violet-blue	Su	N D	3	rough-textured leaves
Scabiosa columbaria	40cm/16in × 30cm/12in	rosettes	pale lavender	Su	N D	5	
Scabiosa ochroleuca	50cm/20in × 30cm/12in	rosettes	pale yellow	Su	N D	4	
Sedum telephium	40cm/16in × 30cm/12in	clump-forming	dull pink	LSu	N D	4	greyish, fleshy leaves
Stachys officinalis	50cm/20in × 30cm/12in	rosettes	dark pink	Su	M N	4	wavy-edged leaves
Succisa pratensis	60cm/24in × 60cm/24in	rosettes	lavender	LSu	M N	5	
Thymus serpyllum	5cm/2in × 45cm/18in	mat-forming	dark pink	Su	D	5	aromatic leaves
Trifolium pannonicum	90cm/36in × 90cm/36in	clump-forming	pale yellow	Su	M N	5	three-lobed leaves
Trifolium pratense	15cm/6in × 45cm/18in	mat-forming E	reddish pink	ESu	M N	3	three-lobed leaves
Verbascum phoeniceum	60cm/24in × 45cm/18in	rosettes	violet	ESu	D	5	many colour forms
Veronica austriaca ssp. *teucrium*	30cm/12in × 60cm/24in	mat-forming	clear blue	ESu	M N D	5	fresh green foliage
Vicia cracca	80cm/32in × 45cm/18in	climbing	lavender	Su	N	3	divided leaves

Bulbs	Height	Habit	Flowers	Season	Soil	Zone	Remarks
Fritillaria meleagris	30cm/12in	erect	purple, white	Sp	M N	4	linear foliage
Muscari neglectum	15cm/6in	erect	dark blue	LSp	N D	4	grassy foliage
Narcissus poeticus	50cm/20in	erect	white, yellow centre	LSp	N	5	linear foliage

Grasses	Height and spread	Habit	Flowers	Season	Soil	Zone	Remarks
Meadow grasses are generally grown from a seed mix, rather than planted, and few are particularly visual in themselves for individual planting, with the exception of the following							
Briza media	50cm/20in × 30cm/12in	upright	tiny silvery heads	Su	N D	4	excellent in borders

PLANTS FOR GRASSLAND – PRAIRIE

Perennials	Height and spread	Habit	Flowers	Season	Soil	Zone	Remarks
Asclepias tuberosa	80cm/32in × 30cm/12in	upright	orange	Su	N D	4	useful hot, dry soils
Aster azureus	80cm/32in × 30cm/12in	upright	sky-blue	A	N D	4	tolerant of light shade
Aster ericoides	80cm/32in × 30cm/12in	clump-forming	white daisies	LA	N D	3	masses of tiny leaves
Aster laevis	60cm/24in × 30cm/12in	upright	lavender	LSu	M N D	4	narrow leaves
Aster ptarmicoides	60cm/24in × 40cm/16in	compact	white daisies	A	N D	3	
Baptisia australis	150cm/60in × 60cm/24in	bushy	dark blue	ESu	M N	5	glaucous stems

Perennials	Height and spread	Habit	Flowers	Season	Soil	Zone	Remarks
Chelone glabra	90cm/36in × 45cm/18in	erect	pink	LSu	M	3	dislikes drought
Coreopsis tripteris	200cm/80in × 50cm/20in	robust clumps	yellow daisies	Su, A	M N	4	long-flowering
Dodecatheon meadia	25in/10cm × 25cm/10in	low rosettes	pink	ESu	N	5	tolerant of light shade
Echinacea purpurea	150cm/60in × 45cm/18in	erect	purple, brown centres	MSu to A	N	3	showy flowers
Eryngium yuccifolium	120cm/48in × 60cm/24in	rosetted	white	LSu	M N	4	yucca-like foliage
Eupatorium purpureum subsp. maculatum	200–350cm/80–140in × 80cm/32in	upright	soft pink heads	LSu, A	M N	4	good butterfly plant
Filipendula rubra	200cm/80in × 120cm/48in	clump-forming	purple-pink	Su	M	3	elegant foliage
Helenium autumnale	110cm/44in × 45cm/18in	erect clumps	yellow daisies	Su	W M N	4	many hybrids
Heliopsis helianthoides	170cm/68in × 60cm/24in	upright clumps	yellow	Su	M N	4	easy and fast
Iris virginica var. shrevei	80cm/32in × 40cms/16in	upright	blue	LSp	M	5	sword-like leaves
Liatris pycnostachya	110cm/44in × 45cm/18in	upright	purple	Su	M	4	linear leaves
Lupinus perennis	70cm/28in × 70cm/28in	clump	violet, pink, white	ESu	N	4	short-lived
Meum athamanticum	45cm/18in × 30cm/12in	mounded effect	cream umbels	LSp to ESu	N	5	fennel-like
Monarda fistulosa	120cm/48in × 45cm/18in	upright	lavender	LSu	M N D	3	aromatic
Physostegia virginiana	70cm/28in × 60cm/24in	erect	bright pink	Su	M N	4	can be invasive
Pulsatilla patens	30cm/12in × 10cm/4in	clump-forming	white-pink	Sp, ESu	N	5	finely divided leaves
Ratibida pinnata	180cm/72in × 45cm/18in	upright	soft yellow	Msu	N D	3	good on clay
Rudbeckia fulgida	90cm/36in × 45cm/18in	branched stems	orange-yellow daisies	LSu, A	M N	4	long-flowering
Solidago rigida	120cm/48in × 40cm/16in	upright	yellow	LSu, A	M N D	3	not invasive like some
Solidago speciosa	150cm/60in × 40cm/16in	upright	yellow	LSu, A	N D	5	superior 'goldenrod'
Verbena hastata	70cm/28in × 20cm/8in	upright	violet to purple	MSu to A	M N	3	often self-sows
Vernonia fasciculata	200cm/80in × 60cm/24in	upright	crimson-purple	A	M N	3	very late
Veronicastrum virginicum	150cm/60in × 45cm/18in	stiffly upright	white	LSu	M N	4	statuesque plant
Zizia aptera	60cm/24in × 40cm/16in	upright	yellow	Sp	N	3	especially good foliage

Prairie grasses	Height and spread	Habit	Flowers	Season	Soil	Zone	Remarks
Koeleria macrantha	45cm/18in × 23cm/9in	clump-forming	narrowly cylindrical	Su	D	3	very tough
Panicum virgatum	150–200cm/60–80in × 75cm/30in	upright	purple-green	Su, A	M N D	5	good autumn colour
Schizachyium scoparium	110cm/44in × 30cm/12in	dense tufts	wispy, long-awned	LSu, A	N D	3	reddish autumn colour
Sorghastrum nutans	200cm/80in × 60cm/24in	spreading	rich brown	Su, A	N D	3	majestic
Sporobolus heterolepis	100cm/40in × 60cm/24in	compact	very fine seed heads	A	N D	3	good soil stabilizer

Bulbs	Height and spread	Habit	Flowers	Season	Soil	Zone	Remarks
Allium cernuum	60cm/24in × 5cm/2in	erect	deep pink bells	LSu	M N D	3	linear leaves
Camassia quamash	60cm/24in × 5cm/2in	clump-forming	bright blue spikes	LSp	M N	5	linear leaves

PLANTS FOR WETLANDS

Here, more precisely, W = aquatic or permanently waterlogged condition and M = permanently moist soil but with an upper rooting zone above the waterlogged zone

Marginal	Height and spread	Habit	Flowers	Season	Soil	Zone	Remarks
Acorus gramineus	20cm/8in × 15cm/6in	spreading	insignificant	Sp	W	5	grassy foliage
Butomus umbellatus	140cm/56in × 45cm/18in	erect	pink on tall stems	Su	W	5	dislikes alkaline soil
Caltha palustris	40cm/16in × 45cm/18in	spreading	large yellow 'buttercups'	Sp	W M	4	

Marginal	Height and spread	Habit	Flowers	Season	Soil	Zone	Remarks
Cardamine pratensis	25cm/10in × 30cm/12in	rosettes	palest lilac	Sp	M	4	
Carex muskingumensis	80cm/32in × 45cm/18in	spreading E	brown	Su	M	7	bright green tufts
Chrysosplenium alternifolium	20cm/8in × indefinite	spreading	green-yellow	LSp	M	4	dislikes alkaline soil
Darmera peltata 'Nana'	45cm/18in × indefinite	spreading	pink	Sp	W M	6	good foliage
Euphorbia palustris	90cm/36in × 90cm/36in	clump-forming	deep yellow	LSp	M	5	
Filipendula ulmaria	100cm/40in × 60cm/24in	erect	cream, fragrant	Su	M N	3	easy and attractive
Hibiscus moscheutos	80cm/32in × 100cm/36in	erect	large pink flowers	LSu	M	5	
Houttuynia cordata	30cm/12in × indefinite	spreading	green-white	Sp	W M	5	blue-grey leaves
Iris sibirica **	80cm/32in × 60cm/24in	erect	blue-violet	ESu	MN	4	many named varieties
Juncus effusus 'Spiralis'	45cm/18in × 60cm/24in	dense tufts	brown	Su	M Ac	4	spiralled, shiny green stems
Lilium pardalinum	150cm/60in × 40cm/16in	clump-forming	orange-red, maroon spots	Su	M	5	lime-tolerant
Lobelia cardinalis	80cm/32in × 30cm/12in	upright growth	scarlet	LSu	W M N	3	dislikes mild, wet winters
Lobelia siphilitica	100cm/40in × 30cm/12in	erect	blue spikes	Su	M	5	
Mentha cervina	20cm/8in × indefinite	spreading	lilac, white	Su	M	7	scented foliage
Menyanthes trifoliata	30cm/12in × indefinite	creeping	white, fringed	Su	W M	3	palmate leaves
Mimulus guttatus **	30cm/12in × 90cm/36in	rosettes	yellow, spotted	Su	W M N	6	can self-seed intolerably
Myosotis scorpioides	30cm/12in × 30cm/12in	creeping	clear blue, long-flowering	Su	W	4	
Parnassia glauca	25cm/10in × 15cm/6in	rosettes	white	Su	M	3	
Primula florindae	70cm/28in × 90cm/36in	rosettes	yellow, scented	Su	W M N	5	
Salvia uliginosa	200cm/80in × 90cm/36in	branched	clear bright blue	LSu	M	9	
Sanguisorba officinalis	100cm/40in × 60cm/24in	clump-forming	small, dark red heads	Su	W M	4	effective en masse
Trollius europaeus **	50cm/20in × 45cm/18in	clump-forming	golden, globular	ESu	W M	4	various colour forms
Typha minima	60cm/24in × 40cm/16in	upright growth	brown, cylindrical spikes	Su	W	5	strap-like leaves
Valeriana officinalis	90cm/36in × 60cm/24in	clump-forming	palest pink heads	Su	M	5	good with bright colours

Water	Depth and spread	Habit	Flowers	Season	Soil	Zone	Remarks
Eleocharis acicularis	to 60cm/24in deep	grassy look	tiny, white	Su		7	usefully neat
Hottonia palustris	to 60cm/24in deep		pale lilac	Su		5	submerged foliage
Hydrocharis morsus-ranae	floating	water lily like	white	Su		4	
Lemna trisulca	floating	tiny foliage				5	least vigorous 'duckweed'
Nymphaea 'Odorata Minor' **	30cm/12in deep × 40cm/16in		white, fragrant	Su		5	finest minature form

Pygmy forms (10–30cm/4–12in water depth) include: 'Aurora', 'Graziella', 'Pygmaea Helvola', 'Pygmeae Rubra and *Nymphaea tetragona*

Nymphaea 'Moorei'	45-70cm/18-28in × 80cm/32in		pale yellow	Su		5	good, but often misnamed

Small forms (40–75cm/16–30in water depths) include: 'Froebelii', 'Hermine', 'Laydekeri Fulgens', 'William Falconer'

Pontederia cordata	100cm/40in × 60cm/24in	erect	blue spikes	LSu		3	lance-shaped glossy leaves

PLANTS FOR DRY AND EXPOSED HABITATS

Here c = coastal. For plants for heathland, see page 169.

Perennials	Height and spread	Habit	Flowers	Season	Soil	Zone	Remarks
Achillea filipendulina	120cm/48in × 50cm/20in	upright	golden-yellow	Su	D	3	majestic appearance
Anthemis tinctoria	50cm/20in × 50cm/20in	clump-forming	yellow daisies	Su	D	4	can be short-lived
Armeria maritima	20cm/8in × 30cm/12in	clump-forming	white, pink or red	LSp	N D	4	grassy foliage
Asphodeline lutea	70cm/28in × 30cm/12in	rosettes	yellow spikes	ESu	N D	6	grassy grey leaves

Perennials	Height and spread	Habit	Flowers	Season	Soil	Zone	Remarks
Balsamorrhiza sagittata	60cm/24in × 30cm/12in	low clump	large yellow daisy	Sp		4	
Campanula portenschlagiana	10cm/4in × indefinite	spreading	lavender-blue bells	LSp	N D		invasive, but ideal for walls
Centranthus ruber	70cm/28in × 70cm/28in	clump-forming	red pink	Su	N D	5	also white form, seeds strongly
Corydalis lutea	30cm/12in × 30cm/12in	compact clump	soft yellow	Sp to A	N D	5	good wall plant
Dalea purpureum	90cm/36in × 50cm/20in	upright stems	purple pea-like	Su	N D	4	
Dianthus gratianopolitanus	15cm/6in × 40cm/16in	mat-forming	deep pink	Su	N D	3	strongly fragrant
Dictamnus albus	80cm/32in × 60cm/24in	clump-forming	pink, white	ESu	N D	3	aromatic, divided leaves
Erigeron glaucus c	30cm/12in × 45cm/18in	tufted	mauve daisies	LSp	N D	3	glaucous leaves
Erodium carvifolium	30cm/12in × 50cm/20in	mat-forming	red	Sp	N D	7	attractive foliage
Gaillardia aristata	75cm/30in × 60cm/24in	erect, spreading	yellow daisies	Su	N D	8	greyish leaves
Geranium sanguineum	30cm/12in × 30cm/12in	clump-forming	deep pink	ESu	N D	4	many colour forms
Iris unguicularis	30cm/12in × 60cm/24in	upright, spreading	lavender blue	ESp	N D	4	fragrant
Kosteletzkya virginica	120cm/48in × 60cm/24in	upright	pink, white, purple	Su	N D	6	showy, hibiscus-like
Lathyrus maritimus	60cm/24in × 60cm/24in	sprawling	purple	Su	N D	3	very tough
Liatris punctata	80cm/32in × 30cm/12in	clump-forming	pink in spikes	Su	N D	3	linear foliage
Origanum laevigatum	40cm/16in × 45cm/18in	mat-forming	violet	LSu	N D	5	aromatic foliage
Papaver orientale	80cm/32in × 60cm/24in	clump-forming	large red poppies	ESu	N D	4	many cultivars available
Penstemon barbatus	150cm/60in × 30cm/12in	upright	red	Su	N D	3	
Penstemon fruticosus var. *scouleri* **	50cm/20in × 60cm/24in	shrubby	purple	Su	N D	4	
Perovskia atriplicifolia	120cm/48in × 100cm/40in	upright subshrub	blue panicles	LSu	N D	6	grey-white stems
Salvia nemorosa/*S. × superba* vars.	100cm/36in × 45cm/18in	erect, branched	blue, pink, white	ESu	N D	5	good 'theme plants'
Sphaeralcea ambigua	80cm/32in × 60cm/24in	upright stems	orange-red	Su	N D	6	
Stanleya pinnata	160cm/63in × 40cm/16in	bold upright	yellow spike	LSp, ESu	N D	4	very striking
Teucrium chamaedrys	40cm/16in × 50cm/20in	shrubby E	red, purple, white	Su	N D	7	

Shrubs	Height and spread	Habit	Flowers	Season	Soil	Zone	Remarks
Aethionema grandiflorum	30cm/12in × 30cm/12in	branching E	rose-pink clusters	LSp, ESu	N D	7	blue-green leaves
Atriplex canescens c	200cm/80in × 200cm/80in	erect	leafy spikes	Su	D	7	silver-grey stems
Baccharis pilularis c	160cm/63in × 300cm/120in	spreading E	small white fluffy	Su	N D	8	
Ceanothus impressus **	150cm/60in × 250cm/96in	spreading E	dark blue	MSp, LSp	N D	7	
Cistus salvifolius **	70cm/28in × 90cm/36in	bushy E	white	ESu	N D	8	grey-green leaves
Comptonia peregrina c	160cm/63in × 100cm/40cm	spreading	fragrant catkins	Sp	N D	4	distinct ferny foliage
Convolvulus cneorum c	60cm/24in × 90cm/36in	compact, bushy	white	LSp, ESu	N D	8	silver-green leaves
Hippophae rhamnoides c	6m/20ft × 6m/20ft	bushy	orange berries	Sp	M N	3	silver-scaley leaves
Lavandula angustifolia ** c	60cm/24in × 120cm/48in	bushy E	lavender	ESu	N D	5	silver, aromatic
Ligustrum ovalifolium	4m/12ft × 4m/12ft	upright E or semi-E	white	MSu	N	5	shiny black fruits
Myrica pensylvanica c	3m/9ft × 3m/9ft	spreading semi-E	grey berries		N D Ac	1	aromatic foliage
Rhaphiolepis umbellata c	150cm/60in × 150cm/60in	bushy E	white	ESu	M N	8	dark green, leathery leaves
Rosa rugosa c	200cm/80in × 200cm/80in	dense, upright	red, pink, white	Su to A	N	2	wrinkled, dark green leaves
Rosa virginiana c	200cm/80in × indefinite	suckering	pink	Su	D	3	invasive, but valuable
Rosmarinus officinalis	70cm/28in × 90cm/36in	upright, bushy E	blue	Su	N D	8	aromatic foliage
Ruta graveolens	60cm/24in × 75cm/30in	rounded, erect E	small, yellow	Su	N D	5	glaucous, blue-green foliage
Santolina chamaecyparissus	50cm/20in × 100cm/40in	compact, rounded E	yellow	ESu	N D	7	tiny, silvery leaves
Shepherdia argentea c	5m/15ft × 3m/9ft	upright, bushy	small yellow	Sp	D	2	silver foliage

Bulbs	Height and spread	Habit	Flowers	Season	Soil	Zone	Remarks
Allium giganteum **	200cm/80in × 30cm/12in	erect	violet drumsticks	ESu	N D	4	spectacular in groups
Allium oreophilum	10cm/4in × 10cm/4in	erect	reddish pink	ESu	N D	8	best in large groups

Bulbs	Height and spread	Habit	Flowers	Season	Soil	Zone	Remarks
Allium schubertii	50cm/20in × 40cm/16in	upright	dusky mauve	ESu	N D	8	starburst flowers, dry well
Gladiolus communis subsp. *byzantinus*	60cm/24in × 20cm/8in	erect	dark magenta	ESu	N D	7	sword-like leaves
Muscari neglectum **	20cm/8in × 10cm/4in	erect	deep blue	LSp	N D	4	increases well
Nectaroscordum siculum	120cm/48in × 30cm/12in	erect	purple-red & green	ESu	N D	6	good in grass
Tulipa sprengeri **	30cm/12in × 20cm/8in	erect	scarlet	LSp to Esu	N D	4	huge range of similar species

Grasses and sedges	Height and spread	Habit	Flowers	Season	Soil	Zone	Remarks
Aristida purpurea	60cm/24in × 70cm/28in	tufted semi-E	very fine	Su	N D	6	very heat and drought resistant
Carex arenaria	30cm/12in × 40cm/16in	spreading tufts	pale brown	Su	N D	7	binds sand
Elymus magellanicus	15cm/6in × 30cm/12in	mounded tufts	green, drooping	Su	N D	5	blue leaves, short-lived
Eragrostis spectabilis	40cm/16in × 50cm/20in	tufts	airy, purplish-red	Su	N D	5	
Festuca glauca	20cm/8in × 25cm/10in	tight tufts	uninteresting		N D	4	blue foliage
Koeleria cristata	50cm/20in × 50cm/20in	dense tufts	silvery or purplish	Su	N D	2	
Melica ciliata	40cm/16in × 30cm/12in	tufts	fawn 'fox-tails'	Su	N D	5	
Pennisetum orientale	50cm/20in × 50cm/20in	clumps	purplish heads	Su	N D	7	dislikes damp winters
Stipa pulcherrima	100cm/40in × 60cm/24in	tufts	long flower 'tails'	Esu	N D	7	unusual but short season

PLANTS FOR DRY AND EXPOSED HABITATS – HEATHLAND

Perennials & small shrubs	Height and spread	Habit	Flowers	Season	Soil	Zone	Remarks
Antennaria dioica	10cm/4in × 45cm/18in	carpeting E	pink, on male plants	ESu	N	2	silvery foliage
Arctostaphylos uva-ursi	10cm/4in × 50cm/20in	spreading E	white, red fruit	Su	N Ac	3	glossy foliage
Arnica montana	40cm/16in × 30cm/12in	rosettes	yellow daisies	LSp	M N Ac	6	rather short-lived
Calluna vulgaris	60cm/24in × 75cm/30in	shrubby E	pink, red, white	Su	M N Ac	4	vast choice of varieties
Chamaedaphne calyculata	30cm/12in × 90cm/36in	shrub E	small, white	Sp	N Ac	2	leathery, glossy leaves
Daboecia cantabrica	50cm/20in × 40cm/16in	shrubby E	pink bells	Su	N Ac	5	
Erica carnea	40cm/16in × 55cm/22in	shrubby E	red, pink, white	LW, ESp	N D	5	lime-tolerant, many varieties
Erica ciliaris	30cm/12in × 50cm/20in	dwarf, shrubby E	bright pink	Su	N Ac	7	
Gaultheria cuneata	30cm/12in × 100cm/40in	dwarf, shrubby E	white berries	Su	N Ac	6	textured leaves
Gaultheria procumbens	15cm/6in × 100cm/40in	mat-forming E	white, red fruit	Su	N Ac	4	glossy foliage
Genista tinctoria	60cm/24in × 100cm/40in	dwarf shrub E	yellow, pea-like	Sp, Su	N	5	
Gentiana sino-ornata	5cm/2in × 40cm/16in	mat-forming E	blue trumpets	LSu, A	N Ac	6	rampant in cool conditions
Phyllodoce × caerulea	30cm/12in × 30cm/12in	shrubby E	small, pink bells	LSp	N Ac	3	
Pilosella officinarum	10cm/4in × 30cm/12in	rosettes	yellow daisies	Sp	N	5	hairy leaves
Salix reticulata	5cm/2in × 30cm/12in	mat-forming	tiny catkins	Sp	N	1	likes cool conditions
Vaccinium vitis-idaea	20cm/8in × 30cm/12in	creeping shrub E	white, red fruit	Su	N Ac	2	small, glossy leaves
Vaccinium angustifolium **	100cm/40in × 100cm/40in	shrub E	white, blue fruit	Su	N Ac	5	
Zenobia pulverulenta	150cm/60in × 100cm/40in	shrub E	white		M N Ac	2	attractive glaucous foliage

Grasses and sedges	Height and spread	Habit	Flowers	Season	Soil	Zone	Remarks
These grasses and sedges will also flourish in normal garden conditions							
Carex testacea	40cm/16in × 40cm/16in	dense tufts E	brown spikes	Su	M N	7	yellow-brown foliage
Deschampsia flexuosa	50cm/20in × 30cm/12in	tufts E	airy panicles	Su	N Ac	4	fine leaves
Festuca ovina **	30cm/12in × 25cm/10in	low tufts E	blue-green	Su	M N	4	grey-green leaves
Koeleria glauca	30cm/12in × 30cm/12in	spreading tufts E	tight fawn heads	ESu	D	4	blue-green leaves
Molinia caerulea	to 240cm/96in × 150cm/60in	dense tufts	purplish panicles	LSu to EW	M N	5	dislikes very limy soils

Grasses and sedges	Height and spread	Habit	Flowers	Season	Soil	Zone	Remarks
M.c. 'Dauerstrahl'	90cm/36in × 90cm/36in	stiff upright	dark purple-brown	LSu to EW	M N	5	yellow stems
M.c. 'Edith Dudszus'	90cm/36in × 90cm/36in	upright	dark purple	LSu to EW	M N	5	
M.c. 'Moorflamme'	75cm/20in × 60cm/24in	arching	dark purple	LSu to EW	M N	5	good autumn foliage
M.c. 'Moorhexe'	90cm/36in × 60cm/24in	strongly erect	very dark purple	LSu to EW	M N	5	dark green foliage
M.c. 'Overdam'	60cm/24in × 30cm/12in	stiff	purple	LSu to EW	M N	5	spiky appearance

Bog	Height and spread	Habit	Flowers	Season	Soil	Zone	Remarks
Andromeda glaucophylla	30cm/12in × 60cm/24in	spreading E	white,	Sp	W M Ac	2	shrub, neat narrow leaves
Drosera rotundifolia **	10cm/4in × 10cm/4in	rosettes E	white, cream, pink	Sp to A	W Ac	9	insectivorous plant
Erica tetralix	30cm/12in × 50cm/20in	shrubby E	pale pink	Su to A	M N Ac	3	small shrub, greyish foliage
Eriophorum angustifolium	30cm/12in × 20cm/8in	tufted	white cottony heads	ESu	W M Ac	2	sedge, needs acid conditions
Kalmia angustifolia f. *rubra*	70cm/28in × 150cm/60in	shrub E	pink, in bunches	ESu	M N Ac	2	shrub
Ledum groenlandicum	70cm/28in × 120cm/48in	dense, shrubby E	white	LSp	M N Ac	2	shrub
Narthecium ossifragum	30cm/12in × 20cm/8in	upright spikes	yellow	MSu	W M Ac	3	herbaceous plant
Pinguicula grandiflora **	15cm/6in × 10cm/4in	rosettes	blue, purple	Su	W Ac	7	insectivorous plant
Polytrichum commune **	20cm/8in	upright, clumping E			M	2	large moss
Sarracenia purpurea **	15–50cm/6–20in	erect	pink to crimson	Sp	W Ac	6	insectivorous plant
Sphagnum capillifolium **	10cm/4in	upright, clumping E			W Ac	1	bog moss
Utricularia vulgaris **	25cm/10in × 20cm/8in	spreading	yellow, cream	Su	W Ac	5	insectivorous

PLANTS FOR OPEN BORDERS

Large perennials	Height and spread	Habit	Flowers	Season	Soil	Zone	Remarks
There are a number of larger perennials of such elegance or 'presence' that they are worth finding space for in even the smallest garden							
Cirsium rivulare 'Atropurpureum'	70cm/28in × 60cm/24in	clumps	deep crimson	Su	M N	4	prickly leaves
Ligularia przewalskii **	100–200cm/ 40–80in × 100cm/40in	erect clumps	yellow, orange	Su	M N	4	good foliage
Macleaya cordata	250cm/100in × 100cm/40in	spreading	flesh-coloured	ESu	M N	4	elegant foliage
Persicaria amplexicaulis	120cm/48in × 120cm/48in	clump-forming	deep pink	LSu	M N	5	several varieties
Rodgersia aesculifolia **	150cm/60in × 90cm/36in	clump-forming	white, pink, red	Su, LSu	M	5	handsome foliage

Smaller perennials	Height and spread	Habit	Flowers	Season	Soil	Zone	Remarks
Achillea hybrids	60cm/24in × 60cm/24in	mat-forming	pink, yellow, white	Su	M N D	3	ferny foliage
Adenophora khasiana **	80cm/32in × 50cm/20in	upright	lavender	Su	N	3–4	campanula-like
Agastache foeniculum	90cm/36in × 30cm/12in	erect, bushy	blue spikes	Su, A	M N	8	aniseed-scented
Alchemilla erythropoda	20cm/8in × 30cm/12in	clump-forming	yellowish-green	LSp, Su	M N D	4	blue-green foliage
Amsonia tabernaemontana	60cm/24in × 45cm/18in	clump-forming	pale blue panicles	LSp, Su	M N	8	
Anaphalis triplinervis **	50cm/20in × 60cm/24in	upright, clumps	white 'everlastings'	Su	N	3	silvery foliage
Artemisia lactiflora	150cm/60in × 60cm/24in	erect	cream	MSu	M N	4	easy and effective
Aster lateriflorus **	120cm/48in × 30cm/12in	clumps	almost white	LSu, A	M	3	spreading branches
Aster turbinellus	120cm/48in × 60cm/24in	erect clumps	lilac panicles	A	M N	5	elegant
Athamanta turbith	60cm/24in × 40cm/16in	clump-forming	white umbels	Su	M N	6	finely divided foliage
Dactylorhiza foliosa	40cm/16in × 15cm/6in	erect	pink to purple	LSp, ESu	M	6	fleshy leaves
Dictamnus albus	80cm/32in × 60cm/24in	erect	white, pink	ESu	N D	3	aromatic foliage
Dierama pulcherrimum	100cm/40in × 60cm/24in	large tufts	pink pendent bells	MSu	M N	8	linear foliage
Epilobium angustifolium var. *album*	150cm/60in × 100cm/40in	spreading	white spires	Su	M N D	6	self-seeds
Erigeron speciosus	60cm/24in × 60cm/24in	clump-forming	lavender-blue	ESu, MSu	M N	3	many varieties
Eryngium agavifolium	100cm/40in × 60cm/24in	rosettes E	greenish white	LSu	N D	7	dramatic spiny leaves

Smaller perennials	Height and spread	Habit	Flowers	Season	Soil	Zone	Remarks
Eupatorium coelestinum	100cm/40in × 40cm/16in	upright	lavender	Su, A	M N	7	fluffy flower heads
Euphorbia polychroma	40cm/16in × 60cm/24in	compact clumps	yellow-green	LSp	N D	4	
Euphorbia schillingii	100cm/40in × 30cm/12in	erect clumps	yellow-green	MSu	M N	5	
Foeniculum vulgare	150cm/60in × 45cm/18in	robust clumps	yellow-green	Su	N D	4	very finely divided foliage
Geranium psilostemon	90cm/36in × 60cm/24in	upright, bushy	magenta	ESu	M N	4	
Geranium wlassovianum	60cm/24in × 60cm/24in	clump-forming	mauve	Su, A	M N	3	
Helianthus 'Lemon Queen'	180cm/72in × 120cm/48in	spreading	soft yellow	LSu to A	M N	5	quick to establish
Hemerocallis citrina	120cm/48in × 75cm/30in	clump-forming	pale yellow	MSu	M N	4	long, arching leaves
Hemerocallis 'Golden Chimes'	90cm/36in × 45cm/18in	clump-forming E	deep yellow	ESu	M N	4	long, arching leaves
Inula ensifolia	40cm/16in × 30cm/12in	bushy	yellow daisies	Su	N D	4	
Lavatera cachemiriana	180cm/72in × 90cm/36in	shrubby	rose-pink	Su	N D	8	
Leucanthemella serotina	150cm/60in × 90cm/36in	robust clumps	white daisies	A	M N	4	very late flowers
Limonium gmelinii	60cm/24in × 40cm/16in	rosettes	blue, violet	Su	N D	4	
Lysimachia ephemerum	100cm/40in × 30cm/12in	erect clumps	white spikes	ESu, MSu	M N	7	grey-green leaves
Lythrum virgatum	90cm/36in × 45cm/18in	erect, branching	purple-red spikes	ESu, LSu	M	3	
Meum athamanticum	40cm/16in × 30cm/12in	clump-forming	small, white	Su	N D	7	aromatic leaves
Nepeta × faassenii	50cm/20in × 50cm/20in	erect, branching	pale blue	ESu, A	N D	3	silvery foliage
Nepeta sibirica	90cm/36in × 45cm/18in	erect, branching	lavender blue	MSu, LSu	N D	3	aromatic leaves
Parahebe perfoliata	60cm/24in × 45cm/18in	shrubby E	blue	Su	N D	9	interesting foliage
Peucedanum verticillare	200cm/80in × 40cm/16in	upright	green yellow	Msu to Lsu	M N	7	stately umbellifer
Phlomis tuberosa	150cm/60in × 30cm/12in	upright	mauve	Su	N D	6	large textured leaves
Potentilla atrosanguinea	60cm/24in × 60cm/24in	sprawling stems	yellow, orange, red	Su to A	N D	5	silvery foliage
Rudbeckia maxima	190cm/76in × 40cm/16in	clump-forming	yellow, black centres	LSu	M N	6	very dramatic leaves
Salvia verticillata 'Purple Rain'	60cm/24in × 45cm/18in	compact clumps	dusky purple	Su	N D	6	exceptional colour
Sanguisorba tenuifolia	120cm/48in × 60cm/24in	spreading	white to purple	LSu	M N	4	elegant divided foliage
Schizostylis coccinea	60cm/24in × 30cm/12in	clump-forming	scarlet	A	M N	6	grassy leaves
Scutellaria incana	60cm/24in × 30cm/12in	upright	soft blue	Lsu to EA	N	5	grey foliage
Serratula seoanei	30cm/12in × 25cm/10in	compact clumps	violet-purple	MA to LA	N	5	useful for late colour
Solidago 'Goldenmosa'	75cm/30in × 45cm/18in	erect clumps	yellow panicles	LSu, A	N D	4	
Solidago rugosa	100cm/40in × 60cm/24in	erect clumps	yellow panicles	A	N	3	the finest 'goldenrod'
Stachys macrantha 'Superba'	60cm/24in × 30cm/12in	erect	pinkish purple	Su	N	4	grey-green leaves
Teucrium hircanicum	70cm/28in × 90cm/36in	erect	red-purple	Su	N D	6	sage-like, aromatic
Thalictrum aquilegiifolium	100cm/40in × 45cm/18in	clump-forming	fluffy pink heads	ESu	M N	5	elegantly divided leaves
Thalictrum polygamum	160cm/64in × 30cm/12in	upright single stems	creamy	Esu to Msu	M N	3	
Thermopsis villosa **	120cm/48in × 60cm/24in	spreading	yellow, lupin-like	ESu	N D	3	three-lobed leaves
Veratrum nigrum	100cm/40in × 60cm/24in	rhizomatous	red-brown panicles	MSu, LSu	M N	6	pleated leaves
Verbesina alternifolia	200cm/80in × 50cm/20in	upright	pale yellow daisies	Su	N D	4	good on poor soil
Veronica longifolia	80cm/32in × 30cm/12in	upright, clumping	pale blue spikes	Su	M N	4	good with deep pinks
Veronica spicata 'Spitzentraum'	50cm/20in × 30cm/12in	upright	true blue	ESu to EA	N	4	greyish foliage
Viola cornuta	15cm/6in × 40cm/16in	spreading E	pale to deep blue	LSp, Su	M N	5	lightly scented

Short-lived perennials	Height and spread	Habit	Flowers	Season	Soil	Zone	Remarks
Achillea hybrids	50cm/20in × 40cm/16in	mat-like clumps	red, pink, yellow umbels	Su	N D	3	flowers fade attractively
Anthemis tinctoria	50cm/20in × 50cm/20in	clump-forming	yellow daisies	Su	N D	4	finely divided leaves
Gaura lindheimeri	60cm/24in × 60cm/24in	lax	white, prolific	LSu	N D	7	rambling wand-like stems
Linaria purpurea	60cm/24in × 30cm/12in	erect	small purple	Su	N D	5	greyish leaves, self-seeds
Lychnis chalcedonica	100cm/40in × 30cm/12in	stiff, erect	scarlet	ESu, MSu	M N	4	usually self-seeds

Short-lived perennials	Height and spread	Habit	Flowers	Season	Soil	Zone	Remarks
Malva sylvestris	100cm/40in × 60cm/24in	sprawling	large, showy pink	Su	N D	5	may self-seed
Verbena bonariensis	110cm/44in × 45cm/18in	upright	violet heads	LSu	N	9	excellent butterfly plant

Bulbs	Height and spread	Habit	Flowers	Season	Soil	Zone	Remarks
Allium sphaerocephalon	90cm/36in × 8cm/3in	slender, erect	dark red globes	ESu	N D	5	
Nectaroscordum bulgaricum	120cm48in × 10cm/4inerect	greenish, purple tips	ESu	N D	6	subtle but striking	

Grasses	Height and spread	Habit	Flowers	Season	Soil	Zone	Remarks
Bouteloua gracilis	60cm/24in × 30cm/12in	clump-forming	brownish-purple	Su	N D	3	
Briza media	40cm/16in × 30cm/12in	clump-forming	purplish panicles	LSp, Su	N D	5	small pendant heads
Calamagrostis × acutiflora 'Karl Foerster'	180cm/72in × 70cm/28in	erect, clumps	pink-bronze	MSu, LSu	N D	7	good vertical interest
Eragrostis curvula	120cm/48in × 120cm/48in	dense tufts	olive-grey panicles	LSu, A	N D	7	
Festuca mairei	100cm/40in × 75cm/30in	tufts	grey-green	Su	N	7	
Hakonechloa macra	35cm/14in × 40cm/16in	arching mounds	yellow-green	LSu, A	M N	5	good foliage
Melica ciliata	70cm/28in × 45cm/18in	loose tufts	pale brown/fawn	ESu, MSu	N D	5	tight flower heads
Miscanthus sinensis 'Afrika'	160cm/64in × 100cm/40in	robust clumps		LSu, A	M N	7	good autumn colour
M.s. 'Kleine Fontäne'	160cm/64in × 100cm/40in	robust clumps	reddish then silver	LSu, A	M N	6	early to flower
M.s. 'Kleine Silberspinne'	160cm/64in × 100cm/40in	robust clumps	silver grey	LSu, A	M N	6	abundant flowers
M.s. 'Nippon'	150cm/60in × 100cm/40in	robust clumps	brownish	LSu, A	M N	6	copper in autumn
M.s. 'Yakushima Dwarf'	100cm/40in × 75cm/30in	robust clumps	pinky-brown	LSu, A	M N	6	the smallest
Sesleria nitida	60cm/24in × 40cm/16in	dense mounds	whitish green	LSp, ESu	N D	6	grey-blue foliage
Spodiopogon sibiricus	150cm/60in × 40cm/16in	upright	hairy panicles	LSu, A	N D	7	bold leaves
Stipa brachytricha	120cm/48in × 80/30in	upright	pinky-grey heads	LSu, A	N	6	
Stipa calamagrostis	100cm/40in × 75cm/30in	dense mounds	silvery buff	Su	N D	7	free-flowering
Stipa tenuissima	40cm/16in × 25cm/10in	dense tufts	green-white to buff	ESu, MSu	N D	7	very delicate appearance

Annual grasses	Height and spread	Habit	Flowers	Season	Soil	Zone	Remarks
Agrostis nebulosa	40cm/16in × 30cm/12in	loose tufts	large, light, airy heads	Su	N		
Briza maxima	40cm/16in × 15cm/6in	erect tufts	large nodding heads	LSp to LSu	N		very distinctive
Hordeum jubatum	30cm/16in × 15cm/6in	dense tufts	green, flushed red	ESu, MSu	N		foliage arching, light green
Lagurus ovatus	50cm/20in x 30cm/12in	tufts	purple tinged	Su	N D		foliage arching, pale green
Panicum capillare	80cm/32in × 60cm/24in	loose tufts	greenish brown	LSu, A	N		
Panicum milliaceum	90cm/36in × 23cm/9in	clump-forming	purple tinged	LSu	N		
Pennisetum setaceum	100cm/40in × 45cm/18in	mound-forming	purplish pink	MSu, A	N D		fluffy seed heads

Flowering annuals	Height and spread	Habit	Flowers	Season	Soil	Zone	Remarks
Agrostemma githago	100cm/40in × 30cm/12in	erect	mauve	Su	N		self-seeds prodigiously
Ammi majus	60cm/24in × 30cm/12in	branching	white umbels	Su	M N		finely toothed leaves
Argemone mexicana	100cm/40in × 30cm/12in	clump-forming	yellow poppies	LSu	D		prickly leaves
Atriplex hortensis var. *rubra*	120cm/48in × 30cm/12in	erect	red-brown/green	Su	M N		purple-brown leaves
Borago officinalis	40cm/16in × 45cm/18in	branching	clear blue	ESu	N D		coarsely hairy
Bupleurum rotundifolium	50cm/20in × 30cm/12in	erect	greenish-yellow	Su	N		stem-clasping, glaucous leaves
Calendula officinalis	50cm/20in × 30cm/12in	loose clump	cream to orange	Su to A	N D		many cultivars available
Centaurea cyanus	80cm/32in × 15cm/6in	erect	dark blue heads	Su	N D		sparse foliage
Claytonia sibirica	40cm/16in × 30cm/12in	spreading	white to pink	Su	M		succulent leaves
Collinsia grandiflora	20cm/8in × 25cm/10in	bushy	pinkish purple	Sp to Su	M N		
Collomia biflora	60cm/24in × 45cm/18in	erect	scarlet	Su	N		softly hairy leaves

Flowering annuals	Height and spread	Habit	Flowers	Season	Soil	Zone	Remarks
Consolida regalis 'Blue Cloud'	50cm/20in × 30cm/12in	branching	bright blue	Su	N		feathery foliage
Coreopsis tinctoria	90cm/36in × 40cm/16in	erect	yellow, red centres	Su	N D		feathery foliage
Cosmos bipinnatus	150cm/60in × 45cm/18in	branching	white, pink, crimson	Su	N		finely cut foliage
Cosmos sulphureus	120cm/48in × 45cm/18in	bushy	orange, black centre	Su	N		
Cynoglossum amabile	40cm/16in × 30cm/12in	greyish	clear blue	ESu	M N		tolerates some shade
Eschscholzia californica	30cm/12in × 15cm/6in	mat-forming	orange, poppy-like	Su to A	N D		feathery foliage
Iberis umbellata	20cm/8in × 25cm/10in	mound-forming	white, pink, crimson	Sp to Su	N		scented flowers
Limnanthes douglasii	15cm/6in × 15cm/6in	spreading	white and yellow	Su	N D		readily self-seeds
Linaria marrocana	30cm/12in × 15cm/6in	erect	violet-purple	Su	N D		many colour forms
Linum grandiflorum var. *rubrum*	40cm/16in × 15cm/6in	erect, slender	dark red	Su	N		greyish leaves
Linum usitatissimum	100cm/40in × 10cm/4in	erect	blue	Su	N		grey leaves
Lupinus subcarnosus	40cm/16in × 60cm/24in	decumbent	purple-blue spikes	Sp	N D		softly hairy palmate leaves
Nemophila menziesii	20cm/8in × 30cm/12in	spreading	bright blue, dark spots	Su	N		hairy leaves, fleshy stems
Nicandra physalodes	90cm/36in × 330cm/12in	erect	violet-blue	Su to A	N		flowers followed by berries
Nigella damascena	40cm/16in × 23cm/9in	erect	blue, pink, white	Su	N		finely divided leaves
Papaver commutatum	45cm/18in × 15cm/6in	branching	bright red	Su	N D		downy, divided leaves
Papaver rhoeas	60cm/24in × 30cm/12in	branching	scarlet	Su	N D		divided, hairy leaves
Papaver somniferum	100cm/40in × 30cm/12in	erect	red, pink, white, purple	Su	N D		greyish, fleshy leaves
Phacelia tanacetifolia	90cm/36in × 45cm/18in	erect	lavender	ESu	N D		dark leaves
Reseda odorata	45cm/18in × 23cm/9in	erect	yellowish green	Su to EA	N D		highly fragrant flowers
Rudbeckia hirta	30cm/12in × 30cm/12in	branching	yellow	Su	N D		often self-seeds freely
Scabiosa atropurpurea	80cm/32in × 23cm/9in	erect, bushy	very dark red	Su	N		stem leaves lobed
Scabiosa prolifera	60cm/24in × 30cm/12in	erect	cream	Su	N		attractive to butterflies
Viola tricolor	8cm/3in × 10cm/4in	spreading	violet and yellow	Sp to A	M N		flowers variable in colour
Xanthophthalmum segetum	80cm/32in × 30cm/12in	erect	yellow daisies	Su	N		lobed leaves
Zinnia peruviana	90cm/36in × 40cm/16in	erect	scarlet, yellow daisies	Su	N		stems become yellow or purple

Biennials	Height and spread	Habit	Flowers	Season	Soil	Zone	Remarks
Borago pygmaea	60cm/24in × 60cm/24in	rosette-forming	clear pale blue	ESu to Ea	M N	7	hairy stems and leaves
Corydalis cheilanthifolia	30cm/12in × 25cm/10in	rosette-forming	deep yellow	Sp to Su	N	6	bronze-tinted, fern-like foliage
Dipsacus fullonum	150cm/60in × 60cm/24in	rosette-forming	thistle-like	Su	N D	3	elegant in winter
Echium russicum	60cm/24in × 60cm/24in	erect	dark red spike	Su	D	3	
Echium vulgare	70cm/28in × 30cm/12in	bushy	deep blue spikes	Su	D	3	usually seeds
Eryngium giganteum	110cm/44in × 30cm/12in	basal rosette	white, thistle-like	Su	N	6	spiny leaves
Hesperis matronalis	90cm/36in × 45cm/18in	rosette-forming	lilac, white, purple	LSp to MSu	N	3	fragrant flowers
Lychnis coronaria	80cm/32in × 45cm/18in	erect	magenta, white, pink	ESu	N	4	grey, woolly leaves
Myosotis sylvatica	20cm/8in × 15cm/6in	tufted	blue, white, pink	Sp, ESu	N	5	self-seeds freely
Oenothera fruticosa	80cm/32in × 30cm/12in	upright	yellow discs	Su	N D	3	evening primrose
Pastinaca sativa	100cm/40in × 30cm/12in	erect	yellow umbels	Su	N	3	wild parsnip
Petroselinum crispum	60cm/24in × 30cm/12in	erect	yellow umbels	Su	M N	3	wild parsley
Salvia sclarea var. *turkestanica*	120cm/48in × 30cm/12in	erect, branched	large pinky-white spike	Su	N D	5	large, coarse, furry leaves
Silybum marianum	100cm/40in × 60cm/24in	rosette-forming	spiny purple thistles	Su	N	7	white-streaked leaves
Smyrnium perfoliatum	100cm/40in × 60cm/24in	erect	greeny yellow heads	LSp	N	6	good buffer colour
Tanacetum parthenium	50cm/20in × 30cm/12in	bushy	white, yellow centre	Su	N D	6	aromatic
Verbascum nigrum	90cm/36in × 60cm/24in	rosette-forming	dark yellow spikes	MSu to EA	N D	5	

FURTHER READING

General

Dutton, Geoffrey, *Some Branch Against the Sky*, David and Charles, Devon, and Timber Press, Portland, Oregon, 1997

Hansen, Richard, and Stahl, Friedrich, *Perennials and their Garden Habitats*, Cambridge University Press, Cambridge, 1993 (an invaluable if technical reference)

King, Michael, and Oudolf, Piet, *Gardening with Grasses*, Frances Lincoln, London and Timber Press, Portland, Oregon, 1996

Kingsbury, Noël, *The New Perennial Garden*, Frances Lincoln, London,1996

Oudolf, Piet, and Gerritsen, Henk, *Dream Plants for the Natural Garden*, Frances Lincoln, London, and Timber Press, Portland, Oregon, 2001

Schenk, George, *Moss Gardening*, Timber Press, Portland, Oregon, 1997

Thompson, Peter, *The Self-sustaining Garden*, Batsford, London, 1997

Wildlife gardening

Baines, Chris, *How to Make a Wildlife Garden*, Frances Lincoln, London, 1994

Stein, Sara, *Noah's Garden*, Houghton Mifflin, New York, 1993

There are also many books about growing wild flora specific to particular regions.

INDEX

References to captions for illustrations are in *italics*.

ACKNOWLEDGMENTS

AUTHOR'S ACKNOWLEDGMENTS

I owe a great deal to the many people over the years who have been very generous with their time and hospitality in explaining their gardens, plantings and landscape philosophies to me: Eva and Roland Gustavsson in Sweden, Uschi Gräfen, Urs Walser, Norbert Kuhn, Philipp Schönfeld in Germany, Sabine Plenk and Heinz Wiesbauer in Austria, Leo Den Dulk and Rob Leopold in the Netherlands, Darrel Morrison of Athens, Georgia, and my colleagues at Sheffield University, James Hitchmough and Nigel Dunnett. Thanks also to those who have been very generous with their hospitality and in supplying contacts for research: Helen and Jonathan Barnes, Piet and Anja Oudolf, and Nancy and Cliff Goldman.

I should also acknowledge the work of the team at Frances Lincoln, who made this book possible and who are always a joy to work with; the work of Marianne Majerus, who has done much of the photography for this book, along with that of the other photographers who contributed; and the garden owners without whom this book would have been unillustrated.

Finally, thanks to my agent, Fiona Lindsay of Limelight Management, and to the constant love and support of my partner, Jo Eliot.

PHOTOGRAPHIC ACKNOWLEDGMENTS

a = above b = below c = centre l = left r = right d. = designer

Mark Bolton 96al (Mary Martin, St Dominic, Cornwall)

Nicola Browne 43, 127 (d. Dan Pearson); 68 (d. Bertil Hansson); 113 (d. Arends Nursery); 145

Nigel Dunnett 67, 74–5, 80 (d. Nigel Dunnett)

John Glover 10; 14–15 (Strybing Arboretum, San Francisco); 25a (the Anchorage, Kent); 38 (Huize Vechtoever, the Netherlands); 57 (Chelsea 2000, d. Upward/Mercer); 104–5 (private garden, California); 111 (Thursley Lodge, Surrey, d. Fiona Laurenson); 118 (Derek Jarman's garden, Dungeness, Kent); 152 (Parham, Sussex)

Sunniva Harte 2 (Waddoup-Wagner, Portland); 6 (Northwest Garden Nursery, Eugene, Oregon); 16, 17 (Sean Hogan); 78 (Somerset Lodge); 96bl (Merriments Garden)

Saxon Holt 27 (Mt. Cuba, Delaware); 87 (back yard, Prairie Garden, Wisconsin); 90 (front yard, Prairie Garden, Wisconsin); 114 (La Tourette Garden, Northern California); 115 (Fleming Garden, Northern California)

Andrea Jones 50–51 (garden courtesy of Roland and EvaGustavsson, Sweden); 86a (Sheffield garden, planting by Nigel Dunnett); 94 (reclaimed garden courtesy of the Speckhardt family, Germany); 106 (coastal garden, Winchelsea, courtesy of Channel 4 Garden Doctors); 122 (Hermanshof Garden, Germany); 140 (Nigel Dunnett's garden, Sheffield)

Andrew Lawson 32a (the Dower House, Morville, d. Kathy Swift); 45, 73bl, 143 (d. Dan Pearson); 83; 96br; 112 (Lady Farm, Somerset)

Marianne Majerus 1, 123b, 148, 150 (d. Noel Kingsbury); 9; 12, 138 (d. Declan Buckley); 13, 20; 22, 37 (Aldenhaeve, the Netherlands); 23 (d. Henri Regenwetter); 25b, 128–9 (the Garden House, Buckland Monachorum, Devon); 26; 28, 39, 89, 141ar (d. Hans Carlier); 31, 156–7 (d. Johan Heirman); 32b (South African Garden, the Garden House, Buckland Monachorum, Devon); 40, 49; 54 (d. Carol Klein); 55 and 70 (d. James Hazlerigg-Kinlay); 56; 58–9 (Sowley House, Hampshire); 60 (d. Jinny Blom); 61 (the Natural History Museum, London); 62 (d. Peter Sievert); 64–5 (d. Peter Chan); 69 (d. Jill Billington); 71 (d. Mark Brown); 72 (d. Ethne Clarke); 73ar, 102 (De Bikkershof, Utrecht, the Netherlands); 81b, 95 (OASE, Beuningen, the Netherlands); 84–5, 88 (d. Dr Ger Londo); 86b, 146–7 (d. Agnes and Georges Majerus); 92–3, 101 (Sticky Wicket, Dorset); 99, 100; 108 (Hodsock Priory, Nottinghamshire); 109 (University of Cambridge Botanic Garden); 116–17; 119 (Chesil Beach); 120–21 (d. Lee Heykoop); 126, 133, 134, 142al, 151, 154, 158–9

Marion Nickig 96ar

Gary Rogers 76–7, 141al, 142ar

Tim Sandall 139 (d. Ian Hodgson, ©The Garden)

Jane Sebire 79, 91 (James Hitchmough's garden, Sheffield); 136–7 (planted wall, Holland)

Jo Whitworth 8; 11; 36 (Croylands, Romsey, Hampshire); 52–3 (RHS garden, Wisley, Surrey); 66 (Beth Chatto Gardens, Essex); 81a (Holt Farm, Somerset); 82 (Fovant Hut Garden, Salisbury, Wiltshire*); 123a; 124, 131, 132 (Lady Farm, Somerset); 125 (d. Land Art, RHS Hampton Court Flower Show)

Rob Whitworth 5; 144 (the Garden House, Devon, d. Keith Wiley)

Steven Wooster 18–19 (Briar Rose Cottage); 21; 29 (Treecrop Farm); 30 (Priona Garden); 35 (Derreen, Co. Kerry, Ireland); 98 (d. Henk Weijers); 103 (Bellevue Gardens, NZ, d. Vivien Papich); 107 (RHS garden, Hyde Hall, Rettendon, Chelmsford, Essex); 110 (d. Piet Oudolf); 135 (Sticky Wicket, Dorset)

* p. 82 Fovant Hut Garden, Salisbury, Wiltshire was created by garden designer Christina Oates together with her husband Nigel and is open to the public. For details: tel. 01722 714756 or visit www.secretgardendesigns.co.uk.